Praise for *Demolishing*

"Most people end up in despair not from disappoi[nt]ment with pleasure. As I have often observed, the [...] have just experienced what you thought would de[...] down. That's the reality Johnny Hunt examines in [...] book. But thankfully, he also illustrates how God can demolish the strongholds in our lives if we surrender to his grace and wisdom. I have known Johnny for many years and appreciate his candor and passion. His enthusiasm is contagious. His answers are practical. His love for God and people is refreshing, for a person so much in demand."

Ravi Zacharias
Bestselling author and international speaker

"*Demolishing Strongholds* is Pastor Johnny Hunt's best book. But in addition to being his finest effort, this book is interesting, even riveting. Most men will find its message connecting with the reality of where they live. and a multitude will find its content liberating. When a man is being strangled by an anaconda, all he wants to know is how to get loose. If you find yourself wrapped in the squeeze of a habit you cannot break, this volume by Pastor Johnny is a road map out of the war zone."

Paige Patterson
President, Southwestern Baptist Theological Seminary, Fort Worth, TX

"Pastor Johnny has had a heart to help men throughout his entire ministry. This new book will provide practical points to minister to even more. I commend this book and his ministry to you without hesitation."

Frank Page
President, SBC Executive Committee

"Becoming the man God intended you to be begins with leading yourself. The gift found in this book is that you don't need to do it alone. God is with you. For more than 25 years, Pastor Johnny Hunt has poured into tens of thousands of men what they need to demolish the strongholds that hold them back. This book shows you how to live in victory."

Tim DeTellis
President, New Missions

"While Christians cannot be possessed by the devil or demons, they can be oppressed by them. Our refusal to repent of our sins gives the enemy the right to harass us. We develop sinful strongholds that hinder our walk with Christ and our witness for Christ. In this new book, Pastor Johnny Hunt helps all Christians, especially men, to demolish strongholds and walk in freedom. I highly recommend this work from my dear friend."

Steve Gaines, PhD
Senior Pastor, Bellevue Baptist Church, Memphis, TN
President, Southern Baptist Convention

"Johnny Hunt is a man's man who has a life message to men. As men go to war with evil daily, *Demolishing Strongholds* will equip them for this intense personal battle. Freedom awaits the men who will read and practice the biblical principles in this book. Read it individually or with a group of men in your forward march from the victory we have in Christ daily."

Dr. Ronnie Floyd
Senior Pastor, Cross Church, Springdale, AR
Immediate Past President, Southern Baptist Convention

"As John the Baptist had an anointed preaching ministry 'to turn the hearts of fathers to their children,' Johnny Hunt also powerfully speaks into the lives of men, husbands, and fathers. May God use this book to turn men to God so they may walk in freedom and faithfulness."

Pastor Jeff Crook
Blackshear Place Baptist Church. Flowery Branch, GA

"Johnny Hunt is one of the most gifted and passionate preachers I know. He has a real burden for the souls of men, and that passion is reflected in the platform God has given him to speak into the lives of men across America. Furthermore, in all of his ministry, Johnny is committed to the absolute authority of God's Word."

Ken Ham
CEO/President, Answers in Genesis

"*Demolishing Strongholds* needs to be in the library of every Christian man in America. Who more qualified to write this relevant volume than Pastor Johnny, a man who hosts one of the largest annual gatherings of men in North America and is widely recognized for his ability to connect with guys on all levels, from the corporate executive to the blue collar employee. *Demolishing Strongholds* addresses the 'hot button' issues facing today's men, laced with captivating illustrations while packed with the biblical principles that will enable any man to walk in the freedom that Christ offers. It is no understatement to say this is a must-read."

Dr. Steve Hale
Evangelist, Steve Hale Evangelistic Association
Woodstock, GA

"Men are constantly faced with temptation, adversity, and various strongholds in today's culture. In *Demolishing Strongholds*, Pastor Johnny addresses issues men face and establishes a biblical game plan for overcoming them. He is an important voice in our culture on how to minister to and disciple men. Every man should pick up a copy of this book and read it."

Robbie Gallaty
Senior Pastor, Longhollow Baptist Church, Hendersonville, TN
President/Founder, Replicate Ministries

Senior, pastor Greg Laurie
email address
greg@harvest.org

DEMOLISHING STRONGHOLDS

get my mail
delivered by
UPS ground

JOHNNY HUNT

HARVEST HOUSE PUBLISHERS
EUGENE, OREGON

Cover by Bryce Williamson, Eugene, OR

DEMOLISHING STRONGHOLDS
Copyright © 2017 Johnny Hunt
Published by Harvest House Publishers
Eugene, Oregon 97402
www.harvesthousepublishers.com

ISBN 978-0-7369-6937-6 (pbk.)
ISBN 978-0-7369-6938-3 (eBook)

Library of Congress Cataloging-in-Publication Data
Names: Hunt, Johnny M., 1952- author.
Title: Demolishing strongholds / Johnny Hunt.
Description: Eugene, Oregon : Harvest House Publishers, [2017]
Identifiers: LCCN 2016037594| ISBN 9780736969376 (pbk.) | ISBN 9780736969383 (eISBN)
Subjects: LCSH: Christian men—Religious life. | Success—Religious aspects—Christianity.
Classification: LCC BV4528.2 .H86 2017 | DDC 248.8/42— dc23 LC record available at https://lccn.loc.gov/2016037594

Printed in the United States of America

17 18 19 20 21 22 23 24 25 / BP-GL / 10 9 8 7 6 5 4 3

Contents

Introduction

It's Time to Break Free

You want to be a man of integrity. You want to be godly. You want to think biblically, to have your wife or close friends say of you, "I can hardly believe the great changes I see in you!" You *want* that. Maybe you even long for it.

But you struggle. You're not "there" yet, even though you really want to be "there." Somehow, you keep stumbling. Falling. Failing. You feel trapped, stuck in a deep, dark pit with no apparent way out. You try hard to cover up your growing mess, but every day it gets harder and harder. You desperately want to win—but by now you doubt whether you ever could.

This book is for you.

For twenty-five years I've helped men just like you to break out of and even demolish the strongholds that have kept them locked up for far too long. Don't get me wrong; I struggle too! But I know we *can* become the men we've always wanted to be. We *can* become men who win. We *can* learn to do now what will make us glad then.

God wants His promises to become reality in our lives, and in this book I want to help you experience them. If you're struggling

7

with one or more strongholds that are devastating your life, *Demolishing Strongholds* will help you find your way out of that struggle and into a life of winning.

Why Write This Book?

A quarter of a century ago I began to sense that I needed to do my best to influence the men of our church to become all God wanted them to be. I see men as a great, untapped reservoir of supercharged energy for the kingdom of God. The average evangelical church would be a total mess if it were not for godly women stepping up to the plate and taking the lead. I want to see strong, godly men once again taking their God-honoring places of leadership in the family and in the church. And I know married women want the same thing! Every week they tell me they long to have godly husbands who will take the mantle of spiritual leadership and run with it.

Each February at First Baptist Church of Woodstock, we hold a men's conference. Husbands and single guys, grandpas and grandsons, pastors and elders and laymen and thousands of others come from around the country to hear from God's Word and encourage each other to become the men they truly want to be. A few years ago we moved the conference to Super Bowl weekend so that on the last day of our meetings, the guys can enjoy the big game together and go home on a high note.

On Sunday night we begin our evening service with hundreds of men in every aisle of the auditorium, most of them on their faces and saying, "God, help me to be a godly man. Help me make a difference in my family and in my workplace and community!" Scenes like that confirm for me that I need to spend a good chunk of my life investing in men.

I didn't become a Christian myself until I was twenty years old, when God saved me out of a pool hall. I was a high school dropout, a teenage drunk, with no purpose and no direction in life. In fact, I quit high school because I refused to give a public book report.

But God had something better for me to do than shoot pool—and that very fact gives me a passion to help men become the leaders, the husbands, the fathers, the heroes that God means for them to be. If God can do anything with me, then God can do something with you.

I don't know what kind of stronghold has you pinned down, but I want to help you destroy it and then remove it so that it's gone. *Is that really possible?* you may wonder. Yes, it really is. I know it is, because over the past twenty-five years I've seen it happen multiple thousands of times.

And now it's your turn.

1

The Strongholds that Lock You Up

I once met with a nationally known public speaker in the Fortune 500 world. With his wife sitting by his side, he told me, "I get up every morning, spend a good thirty or forty minutes reading Oswald Chambers, and then go back to reading the Word of God. But even while I'm reading, I'm aware mentally of what I plan to do that night. I've had two affairs and I've been getting drunk on a regular basis for a couple of years."

Would it surprise you to hear that this man is at church every time the doors are open? He is, along with untold numbers of other Christian men. Frankly, I don't tell you his sad story because I think he's the exception. He's not. I believe he's the rule.

The fact is, the average Christian man is trapped in a vicious cycle. Maybe at a low point in his life he'll say, "God, I'm so sorry. I want to come clean with You." He does come clean, and for a while he feels better. But soon he begins another downhill slide. Eventually he finds himself right back at the bottom.

Then one Sunday, maybe he hears a great sermon and asks God

to forgive him. He feels better again…but in a week or two, he's back once more where he started.

I know this pattern repeats itself weekly in churches all across America. But I also know something else. I know that this man, and millions of others like him, want to do better. They want to be real men of God. They want to lead their families and pursue their work in a God-honoring, spiritually strong way. But an obstacle keeps getting in their way, something that traps them in a destructive lifestyle that ends up feeling a lot like prison.

The Bible calls this "something" a stronghold. And if a man doesn't deal with the strongholds in his life, he'll end up a long, long way from where he wants to be. Just like Bobby.

Where's Their Daddy?

If you ever come to First Baptist Church Woodstock and worship with me at 8:30 a.m., I'll show you just how serious a problem a stronghold can be. I'll point out a certain family to you. I know exactly where they sit. I can point out the lady, who will have six of her eight children with her. I can turn around and say, "See the two girls sitting next to each other in the choir? They are the other two."

And where's their daddy? Well, that's a long story.

Bobby Apon used to perform with NewSong, one of the leading Christian singing groups in America. But then he got hooked on dial-a-porn 900 numbers. After about 11 p.m., a pretty woman used to come on TV and say something like, "Hello, good-looking. Are you lonely? If you are, call me." I used to think, *Ain't nobody going to call her. If they did, she's not the one who will answer. So why would anybody call?* But half a million calls *a day* did go to 900 dial-a-porn services.

Bobby spent $435 a month calling these numbers. You may say, "He was some weird dude, wasn't he?" No, not really. If you had watched him on stage, you wouldn't have seen anyone in the auditorium more handsome. Nobody there would have had less body fat.

The man stood 6 feet 4 and worked out all the time. They didn't call him Superman for nothing! He had a beautiful wife and eight amazing children. And yet Bobby got hooked on dial-a-porn.

I found out about it after I spoke in Euless, Texas, for a Bible conference, where NewSong had just performed. When the group sang, I heard the crowd start hollering, "Go Jesus!" But when Bobby got out front, it sounded a lot more like "Go Bobby!" On stage, some of his provocative movements really grieved me. I went back to my motel room that night, restless. Every time I woke up, thoughts about the concert dominated my mind.

Early the next morning, I sent Bobby a message: "Could we have a late breakfast?" Please understand, I'm not a confrontational guy. I'd rather dig a ditch or take a whipping than to boldly confront someone; but I felt I was supposed to do exactly that, even though Bobby was not a member of my church. When we met, I told him what I had observed the night before and how my heart felt grieved. I said that I loved him and that the only reason I had brought it up was because I really cared about him.

Bobby did not appreciate my efforts. He got angry and called me legalistic and judgmental. "You ought to concentrate on your own life," he fumed. He didn't hurt me, thank God, although later he told me he wanted to. I felt bad about his reaction and doubted whether I should have said anything.

About two weeks later, Bobby called to request a meeting in my office. When we sat down together, he asked how I knew about his sexual struggles. I told him I didn't know, but I just thought he was on dangerous ground and he could open himself up to a place he probably didn't want to go. That's when he told me about the 900 numbers.

At that time we didn't yet have a ministry in place at Woodstock to work with fallen ministers, and frankly, I didn't even have the knowledge to speak effectively into Bobby's situation. But I sought to get him some help anyway, gave him the best counsel I could, and prayed with him. Then he went on his way.

I didn't see Bobby much after that, except whenever our paths crossed on the road. But within a year or so he came to see me again—this time to confess his adultery. It turned out that through a 900 number, an anonymous woman told him how to find a willing partner for an affair. He then called a girl in another state, where his group had scheduled a concert, and arranged the whole scheme.

I'll never forget what he said in his last visit to my office. "When I left Georgia," he said, "I knew that I planned to be with that lady in a Louisiana hotel room. I've never been unfaithful to my wife, pastor, even though I've been hooked on pornography and I've been greatly tempted."

The Word of God says that when you get involved in lawlessness, it always leads to more lawlessness. Sin is never satisfied with how much of you it has. It always wants more. An old song says that sin will take you farther than you want to go, cost you more than you want to pay, and keep you longer than you want to stay. It plays for keeps. As evangelist Freddie Gage has said, "Sin thrills and then it kills. It fascinates and then it assassinates. If you play, you're going to pay." You get burned every time.

As Bobby crossed the state lines, he said it felt like the Spirit of God said to him, "Don't do it!" But he kept on going. "I remember when I crossed into Alabama," he told me. "I remember when I crossed into Mississippi. I remember when I crossed into Louisiana. I never dreamed it could really happen. Johnny, it was one time only. I've never been involved with her or anybody else in my whole life." He stopped and looked away for a moment. "I can't deal with this," he said softly. "I've got to get this out of my heart so I can go on."

Are you dealing with a stronghold? It may be related to pornography, an affair, or it may be something else entirely. Whatever it is, it's embedded itself in your heart and you feel trapped. You need to know that until you do rip it out of your heart, you can't go on, any more than Bobby could.

Although his adultery had already become known to his wife, I urged Bobby to confess his sin to her. I also told him he needed to get into counseling and start a restoration process.

I hate to say it, but Bobby lost his ministry. The guys in the singing group told him, "You're a very gifted and talented singer, but we just can't have that. You've disqualified yourself from the ministry." They forgave Bobby, but the consequences of his sin cost him his job.

Do you realize there's a difference between forgiveness and consequences? Sometimes people think, *You're just holding this over me. You're not forgiving.* But forgiveness doesn't always wipe out the consequences. I had a staff member who fell into an adulterous relationship with a secretary. God knows I deeply love that man, but I dismissed him. That was the necessary consequence of his sin.

Bobby's wife forgave him and they seemed to be moving on. When the dust finally started to settle, it looked as though Bobby was beginning to grow spiritually and build a stronger relationship with his wife.

But one Sunday night a couple of years later, my phone rang. When I answered, I heard the troubled voice of Bobby's wife. "We want you to know that he's done it again," she said. "Pastor, we're meeting with our own pastor tomorrow morning. Please pray for us. I am devastated." Still, she made it clear she wanted to find a way to save her marriage. I told her I'd be praying for them and asked her to let me know the outcome.

The next day, my phone rang again. This time it was a friend telling me something I never expected to hear. Early that morning, Bobby had told his wife that before their counseling session, he needed to see his doctor. After his doctor visit, he drove to a location near his home and made a decision to end his life.

I officiated at his funeral.

A year or two after Bobby's death, I performed a wedding at which I felt distracted by a teenage girl crying through most of the ceremony. Afterward I found out it was Bobby's oldest daughter, Abigail. She just couldn't stop thinking about her own special day. Who would walk her down the aisle, now that her daddy was gone?

Can you see what drives me to be so passionate about this crucial issue of strongholds? Every Sunday morning when I stand up to preach, I look out at a widow with eight children (they joined our church after Bobby's death). Her husband is in eternity because the devil plays for keeps. Sin took Bobby farther than he wanted to go, cost him more than he wanted to pay, and kept him longer than he wanted to stay. In the name of Jesus Christ of Nazareth, how can we win the war unless men come clean?

Every day of my life, Bobby's tragic story reminds me of the high cost of low living. I loved Bobby. I still consider him a good man— but he allowed himself to get ensnared by the enemy. He permitted a thought to become a habit, which became a deed, and then became a stronghold that took him down. Strongholds destroy our marriages, devastate our children, and lay waste to our personal lives. We have a simple but critical choice to make. Either we learn how to dismantle the strongholds in our lives, or they will dismantle us.

A stronghold begins in the mind. Bobby recognized that—at one point, he said, "The enemy began years and years ago to very subtly lay his trap for me and to pull me away from the things of God." And on another occasion he said, "I want to encourage you to listen to God while it is still a small voice in your heart. Don't make God have to get your attention the hard way."

The Glory Stealer

People today often make fun of a personal devil. We ridicule spiritual warfare. We'd rather read about it than try to understand how to successfully engage in it. But the Bible teaches us a war is being waged that we can't fight in our flesh. It says, "Though we walk in the flesh, we do not war according to the flesh. For the weapons of our warfare are not carnal [that means they're not merely human] but mighty in God for pulling down strongholds" (2 Corinthians 10:4).

When I started doing men's conferences about a quarter of a century ago, I asked the women related to the attendees to pray for me. They would send me letters with statements like these:

> My husband brings home material he wants me to watch and I'm offended by it. I used to play along with that until I got saved and got right with God. He claims he's saved, but he's still trying to bring me into it.

> I want you to know that my husband regularly frequents different bars and strip joints.

A war is raging and many of us aren't prepared or equipped for it. The Bible says we need to deal with our sin lest Satan outwit us, "for we are not unaware of his schemes" (2 Corinthians 2:11).

If you're a believer in Christ, do you understand that Satan seeks to gain an advantage over you? What could it mean that the devil wants an advantage over *you*?

Scripture calls Satan a slanderer, a liar, Lucifer. But do you know what name I'd choose? I'd call him a glory stealer.

The devil could not stand the fact that God was getting all the glory in heaven, so he tried to dethrone the Lord. Six times in Isaiah 14, the devil uses the pronoun, "I," as in, "I will ascend above the throne of the most high." He was saying, "I'm tired of God getting the glory. *I* want to get the glory."

I believe you picked up this book because you want to be a real man of God. You want to be an example to your kids, a hero to your wife, a model for others. When you become a man of God, do you know what God will do with you? God will be glorified in you. When a church obeys God, do you know what that church will do? That church will give God glory.

And what will the devil do? He'll do what he did when he first got kicked out of heaven ages ago. He's still trying to steal the glory of God. He will do everything he can to rob a godly man of his testimony.

I doubt the devil hates you in particular, although he certainly has no fondness for you. But it really isn't about you. Satan hates God, and when God is being glorified through you, the devil wants to do something terrible in your life just so God won't get the glory He deserves. Satan doesn't give a rip about you. He just doesn't want God to be glorified.

Remember what happened in Samson's life when God was being glorified through him? Sultry, seductive Delilah came along. When she finally got Samson to buy into her lies, he first lost his strength and then he lost the victory in his life. As a result, the Philistines threw a festival and gave praise and glory to the moon god, Dagon, for bringing Samson down.

Delilah didn't bring him down. She was just the tool Satan used to dispose of Samson. Our war is not against flesh and blood, but that woman was flesh and blood. She was the means that Satan used to bring about Samson's spiritual destruction. After the episode with Samson, Scripture never mentions Delilah again.

The same thing is true in our world today. No prostitute brought down certain pastors or evangelists. The devil did. No homosexual lover brought down certain leaders. The devil did. No financial scheme brought down those who succumbed to them. The devil did.

The same enemy wants to bring you down. Satan seeks to "gain an advantage" over you and me so that he can steal God's glory.

Prepare for Battle

No one prepares for a battle of which he is unaware. And no one wins a battle for which he doesn't prepare.

I prepare for battle. I really do. I understand that life is not a playground, but a battlefield. So I get prepared.

When I travel back home from a preaching trip to Africa, for example, I usually have to stop somewhere in Europe to spend the night. Since I know that many of the hotels over there program their televisions to show skin flicks as soon as you turn on the TV, I don't turn them on.

The Christian life is not difficult, as you may think. In fact, it's impossible. That's why God never called you to live it; He called you to die and let Christ live it through you. The weapons God gives you are mighty through God, not through you.

You simply cannot fight a spiritual battle with carnal weapons. And that explains why you may be thinking, *Man, I'm going to church again this week. Maybe I'll be forgiven and rededicate my life.* Cycle, cycle, cycle, cycle, cycle. Do you know the problem? You're trying to do the work only God can do.

Listen! You will win only by using the weapons God gives you—weapons that are mighty through Him. He has made them available to you. Your part is to choose to use them. And if you'll use them, you can win this battle. In coming chapters, we'll talk about the most important weapons you'll need.

The Bible instructs you to "be strong in the Lord" (Ephesians 6:10). It doesn't say, "Be strong in the flesh." It doesn't instruct you to be strong-minded, strong-willed, or even strong-intentioned. It tells you to be strong in the Lord and in the power of His might. "Put on the whole armor of God," it says, "that you may be able to stand against the wiles of the devil." The devil is wily and he has some nasty schemes to bring you down. He's got a plan just for you.

God tells us, "Do not give place to the devil" (Ephesians 6:27). The word translated "place" speaks of an opportunity. Don't give the devil an opportunity, even a slight one, to launch his plans against you. If you do, he'll use the opportunity to build a stronghold. And from that stronghold, he'll launch attacks meant to destroy you.

Any Habit that Gets You

During a recent exam, a doctor said to me, "I have to ask these questions, so please don't be offended. Do you drink alcoholic beverages?"

"No, ma'am."

"Do you use tobacco?"

"No."

"Have you ever?"

"Yeah, I used to."

"How long ago?"

"I quit smoking when I was fifteen. I didn't get saved until I was twenty. I didn't quit getting drunk until I was twenty."

That was a long time ago, but I can still remember when somebody would say to me, "Go ahead and smoke one." So I took one. Even if you weren't a Christian, at that point you prayed, "O God, help them not to ask if I inhaled it."

But they did ask. When I'd shake my head, they'd say, "If you really want to start smoking, you *have* to inhale it."

Do you know what it's like to inhale a cigarette for the first few times? I remember, even though it's been half a century since I did it. It's bad because it's unnatural. If it were not unnatural to put smoke in my lungs, I would chase fire engines. I'd rush to fires and try to inhale just enough so that the smoke didn't overcome me.

"Hey, a free smoke! Have a drag."

You take in the smoke, you cough, your eyes get bloodshot, and your ears water. And they say, "Hey, good one."

"Yeah."

"You want another one?"

"No, I'm good."

Do you know what happens then? After a while, you get used to it. And eventually it becomes a habit. And even your smoking friends might say to you, "Hey, man, you're smoking too many of them."

"Oh, give me a break," you reply. "I can quit them anytime I want to."

And you probably could…until the habit becomes a stronghold. And then you have no choice anymore.

Listen: *A stronghold is any habit that got hold of you.*

At one time in your life, you were playing around with it because you didn't see it as a big deal. And then one day, it just kind of closed its grip on you. And now you can't get loose.

That's a stronghold.

Oh, you might experience momentary victory. You might go a week without falling into it. But the truth is, it's got you. And now you feel ashamed that you've let something so small get you. What you once had, now has you. That's called a stronghold.

A stronghold is an enemy fortress erected in your home territory, from which your foe may launch attacks behind your defenses whenever he chooses. If you give place to the devil, you allow him to build a strong fortress deep within your territory. Once it's built, you don't try to ward him off and you don't need the armor of God—you need deliverance. He's already in your life because you've given him place.

When you surrender to his attacks by saying things like "I'm going online to visit some sex sites," or "I'm going to cheat my employees," or "I think I'm going to get me a secret girlfriend"— whatever your surrender looks like—you allow him to build an iron fortress in your life, in your own personal territory. And from there your enemy launches vicious attacks behind your defenses.

How can you win when that happens? How can you be a victorious man of God if you've given the enemy a chunk of your life territory? How can you triumph if you let him build a vast stronghold behind your defenses?

How can you win?

The answer is, you can't.

I know what "winning" looks like in my own life. First, I want to take as many people to heaven with me as I can by introducing them to salvation in Christ. Second, I want to reach my personal God-given potential, whatever the Lord wants to do in me—no holds barred, no human being slowing me down, sky's the limit. Third, I want to help as many people as possible to become fully devoted followers of Jesus Christ.

But how can I accomplish any of those things if I give the devil territory in my life? If I let him build a stronghold behind my defenses, I can't accomplish any of these goals. And if you've allowed the devil to build a stronghold in your life, you can't accomplish any of the things most important to you, either.

Are You in a Rut?

I've visited Alaska several times. Once you leave the main roads, you start to see very high road signs. Why so high? When the snow arrives, the plows push the snow into massive drifts. I once saw a sign about ten feet high that said, "Choose your rut carefully. You'll be in it the next 100 miles."

Are you in a rut?

You can attend all the men's conferences you want to. Go to all the worship services you can. Hear all the good preachers, listen to excellent podcasts—but you're in a rut. A vicious cycle. A stronghold.

And you've been unable to break free of that stronghold. It has you trapped.

I'm telling you, you can be free if you want to be. But many guys just don't want to be free.

I travel to a lot of places and often speak to the same men, time after time. I find a lot of them still in bondage. And I wonder, *Goodness, am I just making them feel better?*

Some men don't live right because they figure that listening to sound preaching is their punishment for their bad living. They think, *My preacher beats me up. He gives me a good whipping every Sunday, but that's just the cost for my lifestyle.* They think they can continue to live like that without consequences.

But that's not true. Their strongholds *will* take them down.

Is that you? Maybe *you* need to be set free. The good news is that you can be free...if you want to be. Winning your freedom, however, requires some important decisions. And the very first one involves your mind.

Part One

How Strongholds Imprison You

2

The Battle for Your Mind

A war is waging for control of your thought life. When you surrender to temptation, your thoughts become deeds, your deeds can become habits, and your habits can become a stronghold. What kinds of weapons does Satan use to build a stronghold? Almost always he will use an attack on the mind. Satan attacks through getting you to believe a lie, which leads to a sinful attitude or action. When you indulge in those attitudes or actions long enough, they turn into habits, which he uses to build strongholds. In this way, he makes a man his servant—and a servant obeys his master.

Fellow pastor Adrian Rogers, a dear brother in Christ who passed on to his eternal reward in 2005, taught me that the devil would rather get you to think wrong than get you to do wrong. Why? Because if you do wrong, you might get right; but if you think wrong, you won't see anything wrong that needs to be set right.

Training our minds to think biblically can feel like a lot of work, however. So sometimes we attempt to bypass that work by trying other strategies. Maybe we move to a new place, change jobs, or surround ourselves with a different environment. A fellow came to my office one day and told me that to escape some persistent temptation, he had traveled to Israel. He thought he'd be safe there, because he was going to walk where Jesus had walked. "I went to Israel twice," he said, "and had an affair there both times."

But think about it—Judas walked in Israel too.

When the devil builds a stronghold in your mind, it doesn't matter if you visit Israel. It doesn't matter if you decide to walk where Jesus walked. It doesn't matter if you buy an old church building and make it your home. When you don't destroy the stronghold, the devil can attack you from within your own territory. Satan launches his attacks from your mind, and since you take your mind with you wherever you go, what difference does it make where on this planet your feet might take you?

The Foundation of All Strongholds

All of Satan's strongholds begin in a shabby and undisciplined thought life. Proverbs 4:23 says, "Keep your heart [or mind] with all diligence, for out of it proceed the issues of life." This is the language of a fighter. "Keep" means "be diligent," fight for it.

Four verses later the writer says, "And keep your eyes looking straight ahead, and don't look off to the right or to the left. And watch that you do not speak perverse things with your mouth." The progression goes from your mind, to your eyes, to your mouth. And then he says, "Keep your feet on the path."

If your mind isn't right, your eyes won't be right, your mouth won't speak right, and your feet won't take you to the right places. A man who allows himself to dwell on wrong thoughts is almost certain to give the devil a gigantic stronghold in the center of his mind.

"As a man thinks in his heart, so is he" (Proverbs 23:7). You are not what you think you are, but what you think, you are. Impure thinking produces inconsistent living. Whoever lacks virtue in his thinking cannot but act indecently. Holy living follows sanctified thinking.

All of this means that the battle for your life is really a battle for your mind. If you want to win, then you must take aim at the real target—your mind.

How God's Word Shapes Your Mind

Repeated, prolonged exposure to God's Word shapes your mind in at least four ways.

1. It exposes the sinfulness of what you are tempted to do.

Sin tries to color itself and camouflage itself so that you don't see it for what it is. The Word of God, however, exposes the sinfulness of what you feel tempted to do. One of Satan's subtle snares is to convince you that sin is really not so bad after all. God's Word, however, allows you to see things for what they really are. When we bring something out of darkness and into the light, it doesn't look near as pretty in His shining presence as it did in the dark.

2. You gain God's viewpoint.

Because many temptations carry a strong emotional punch, you tend to get caught up in your feelings. Once you identify with those feelings, it becomes increasingly difficult to respond correctly. You've been duped.

Because the Bible declares what God thinks about the issues of life, the truth of Scripture allows you to separate yourself just far enough mentally to successfully deal with the temptation. God's Word allows you to see sin for what it is in God's sight.

3. The principle of displacement.

Once a seductive topic enters your mind, it's virtually impossible *not* to think of it unless you purposefully turn your attention elsewhere. When you refocus your thoughts to the Word of God, you turn your attention away from the temptation and toward something productive. That's the strategy presented in Philippians 4:8, which we'll look at a little later. If you don't shift your attention away from the temptation, you may well begin some illicit dialogue in your head, which often goes something like this:

I know I shouldn't do this, but I haven't done it in a long time. I'm really going to hate myself later. But…why not? God will forgive me. And besides, I've already blown it. I'll do it just this once and tomorrow I'll start over.

When you allow such warped mental discussions to continue, you're sunk. The longer you let them go on, the more time the temptation has to settle into your emotions and will.

The old saying is right: The Bible will keep you from sin, or sin will keep you from the Bible. In this age of easy access to the worldwide web, you're just one click away from having real difficulty with forming a biblical mind. What you put in your mind *is* going to affect the way you think about your wife. It's going to affect the way you think about your friends. And it's going to affect the way you view God.

Somebody once asked me, "I'm struggling in [name the area] of my life. What would you do?" I said, "Find every verse that relates to that area and start memorizing a Scripture passage that deals with it. Bring that truth to mind." To effectively combat the onslaught of the enemy, you need an arsenal of verses on the tip of your tongue, verses so familiar to you that they come to mind without any conscious effort.

I'm sixty-three years old. If I can memorize three to five verses of Scripture a week, so can you. Psalm 119:11 says, "Thy word have I hidden in my heart, that I might not sin against You." How can you cleanse your way? By the Word. What do you need in your heart to avoid sin? The Word. So begin memorizing specific scriptures that address the areas that trouble you the most. Get them in your mind. Nail them there. Quote them audibly when you're tempted.

Remember that if the perfect, sinless sovereign Son of God relied on Scripture to pull Him through the temptations Satan threw at Him, what hope do we have without it? If we're going to have a biblical mind, we have to base that mind on biblical truth.

4. You express faith when you turn your attention to it.

When you turn to God's Word, you're saying, "I believe God is able to get me through this." I never want to get to the point where I believe there is something in my life that God can't handle. When you consciously put your attention on the Word of God, you're affirming His limitless power. You're saying, "I believe God is able. He is mightier than the power of sin. He is mightier than my flesh. He is mightier than the world. He is mightier than Satan himself. Greater is He who is in me than he who is in the world" (see 1 John 4:4).

Nothing moves God like the active faith of His people! When you speak the truth out loud, it says you've taken a stand with God against the enemy. When I do this, I often feel a sense of courage and conviction sweeping over me. To be able to speak the truth out loud, though, you need to make a regular practice of reading that truth in God's Word.

But I know how guys think! I've read that a large number of male high school graduates do very little reading after they leave school. But I also know that regular reading of Scripture is a discipline that pays huge dividends.

Right now I'm doing some writing projects beyond what I normally do. I'm not a very good writer, but I'm writing. Why? It's an extremely helpful discipline for me. In fact, most of the things that God has developed and used in my life for His glory and for the good of the body of Christ have not been things that I love, but things that God has worked in my life through discipline.

I'm a high school dropout. After I became a Christian, I was able to return to school to get an education. But before I became saved, I was headed in the opposite direction. I don't naturally love to read. And yet I try to read a minimum of one good book a month, in addition to all the books I use for my studies and writing.

If you say, "I read the Bible, but I don't get anything out of it," then keep reading it until you do get something out of it. I don't want to be ugly, but if you're reading the Bible and getting nothing out of it, that says more about where your heart is than where God is. If the Word seems dry to you, keep reading.

People ask me, "Do you ever read the Bible, have a devotion in the morning and spend time with the Lord, but don't feel like you're getting much out of it?" Of course I do. "Then why do you keep doing it?" I persevere because on some of those dry mornings, God just shows up. It's surreal. It's as though He physically steps into the room. I almost want to say, "Lord, do You want this seat? I'll just sit on the floor." The dry moments are *so* worth it when these spectacular times come!

(By the way, if God came to me every day like that, I'd be ruined. I think this is where some people wander off in their theology. They really think they can usher in God's presence by what they chant or say. Rubbish. And that's all I'm going to say about that.)

Focus Your Mind

When you allow a stronghold to continue unopposed in your life, that stronghold will cause spiritual alienation. Your lack of devotion to God will prevent you from enjoying any intimacy with God. You will have no sense of His power, no sense of Christ's presence in your life or in your worship.

You have no intimacy with the Savior because you're alienated from God. This is a spiritual issue, the direct result of a stronghold caused by unbiblical thinking. It all starts with your mind, with your thinking.

The Bible teems with truth about a man and his thinking. "As a man thinks in his heart, so is he" (Proverbs 23:7). "And do not be conformed to this world, but be transformed by the renewing of your mind, that you may prove what *is* that good and acceptable and perfect will of God" (Romans 12:2).

When your mind is not right, you don't think right and you do hurtful things with your body. Everything's a struggle for you, and the fight only gets more intense the more your thought life is messed up. Jesus wants us to stop compartmentalizing our lives so that He can sweep through every corner of our minds to work fresh in our hearts. I believe that's what we all really want at the end of the day.

The Bible calls us to *focus* our minds. I've always loved Isaiah 50:7, which prophesies that Jesus would set His face like flint when He went to Jerusalem to be crucified. He went there for the express purpose of dying. He set His face like flint to His task—and we need a similar mindset.

Psalm 19:14 says, "Let the words of my mouth and the meditation of my heart be acceptable unto thee, O God, my strength and my Redeemer." The word "acceptable" means "approved in worship." It's an offering you bring to God.

More specifically, it's a warrior's offering.

The Warrior's Concentration

The apostle Paul tells us that if we're going to have a mind fully prepared to help us in our struggles to become the men God would have us to be, we need to meditate on some things. We have to mull them over, take them in, and chew on them. The classic passage on this discipline is found in Philippians 4:8:

> Whatsoever things are true, whatsoever things are noble, whatsoever things are just, whatsoever things are pure, whatsoever things are lovely, whatsoever things are of good report; if there is any virtue, and if there is anything praiseworthy, meditate on these things.

God wants us to suit up so we will develop a biblical mind. The first three things Paul mentions here I'd call "inward armor"—character qualities you develop on the inside, qualities that no one can see just by looking at you, but which directly influence and determine the way you act.

First, Paul uses the word "true" to challenge us to be real. What does it mean to be true? It means to be genuine, sincere, not plastic. It means that you're true to God, you're true to others, and you're true to yourself. Are you true to God? Are you true to others?

Truth is part of the warrior's armor listed in Ephesians 6:14. Paul writes, "Stand fast, having girded your waist with truth." Did you know that a Roman soldier girded his belt down by his groin? I find that fascinating. When a man thinks untrue things, soon his life reflects the falsehoods he has entertained in his mind. And we see that most clearly, perhaps, in the way a man thinks about sex. Are your sexual thoughts true? Or have you allowed the enemy to unbuckle your belt?

Second, the apostle uses the word "noble." The word means to think about honorable things worthy of respect. If it's true that we externalize our thoughts, then honorable thoughts create honorable people. Our thoughts should focus only on things worthy of God—and God "listens" to what we think. To be noble invites reverence. This quality makes a man worthy of respect and dignity. It promotes inner character.

The word also carries the idea of serious as opposed to frivolous. If there's one thing every Christian man ought to be serious about, it's his relationship with God.

Third, Paul encourages us to think about "just" things, referring to that which is right. The word speaks of a right relationship and proper action. We ought to contemplate and think on those things that cause us to be right with God and right with each other. We should be men who face our duty and do it, men whom others can count on because they know we'll do what's right.

The word "just" describes whatever is in perfect harmony with God's unchanging standards as revealed in Scripture. Sometimes when I'm reading the Bible, God reminds me what type of attitude

I ought to have toward someone who normally causes me fits. "Just" means conformable to God's standard, worthy of His approval, righteous as in the eyes of God, morally upright.

A just man wants to do the right thing not merely when it's convenient or when he's being watched, but comprehensively. He's a man of integrity at all times.

Greek grammarian A.T. Robertson said that this verb is in the present tense middle voice, which means *we're* responsible to do this. We're responsible for our thoughts. We can choose to dwell on lofty ideas rather than base ones. It's a choice, a decision that we all must make.

The Warrior's Consideration

Paul's list then moves from inward armor to outward armor, to what others can see when they watch you. Once you put on the inner armor of godly character traits, God wants you to put on the outer armor of proper behavior. And what does this armor look like?

Pure

First, Paul calls it "pure." The underlying Greek term refers to all sorts of purity, including purity in your thoughts (a struggle for us all). But it also speaks of purity in your words and deeds. When you realize that more than one-third of every download on an American computer is pornography, you come to see what a challenge it is to think purely!

How does a person in our day keep his thoughts pure? By excluding the impure. Once given a lodging, impure thoughts are virtually impossible to evict. They lurk in the hidden recesses of the mind and often make their presence known at unexpected times. The late Scotsman John Phillips said that once a person lets his thoughts wander down some impure path, hidden legions joyfully emerge and stampede, pushing the mind into all kinds of sin.

Psalm 119:9 asks, "How can a young man cleanse his way?

By taking heed according to Your word." Note that the psalmist describes only one way to keep pure—through the Word of God. Do you realize that the only offensive weapon a Christian has is the Bible? If you're looking for something other than God's Word to equip you to have a biblical mind, then you might as well hand over to Satan the keys to your mind.

It's not as complicated as we sometimes make it. It's actually pretty simple. If I'm going to think biblically instead of impurely, then I need a biblical mind. And I cannot have a biblical mind without allowing the Bible, the Word of God, to speak into my life.

Lovely

Second, Paul encourages us to think about "lovely" things. Lovely means to be sweet, gracious, generous, and patient. We're not always those things! So when we're not, we acknowledge our fault and repent.

The word "lovely" is often used to describe the fine arts or music. It refers to that which is orderly, the opposite of confusion and disorder. It means beautiful and attractive and refers to that which calls for love. People are attracted to you and your life when it appears lovely.

I know, of course, that no man would say to another, "I am so grateful for my brother here. He's lovely." No, but there's something outwardly attractive about him because God has so worked in his life. It's a word for the winsome, undergirding force that comes from having a vibrant relationship with Jesus. We need to have His sweetness about us!

When our thinking can be described as lovely, then we will build bridges and not barriers. We will throw bouquets and not bombs. We will love and not cause discord. We will be selfless and not controlling. That is a miracle of God.

The third term, "a good report," is pregnant with meaning. It signifies the delicacy that guards the lips—that nothing be expressed that could disturb devotion or cause a scandal. It refers to that which does not offend. It speaks to the capacity to look for something helpful to say, even if you can't agree with everything that's being done. If you have to disagree, you'll do it in such a way that even your disagreement incorporates helpful suggestions. A Christian does not have the luxury of being unkind.

I've gone to airport counters where I've been told that I've been bumped off a flight. I'll say something like, "Do you know my status? Do you know how many miles I've flown? I'm a flying colonel!" And they'll look at me like, "So?" Then I'll say, "This isn't right!" because I'm angry. But of course nobody gets anywhere with that.

So I'll get a Coke, sit down, and think for a moment. And then the Spirit of God will work on me, prompting me to walk back to the counter. As I wait in line, the agent sees me and thinks, *Oh no, trouble is back.* Finally, when it's my turn to step up to the counter I'll say, "Sir, I'm a Christian. I know you never would have known that by the way I just acted, but I'm sorry. I asked God to forgive me, and I'd like to ask for your forgiveness too." Have you ever done anything like that? May God give us a good report.

The Warrior's Contemplation

Paul uses the word "virtue" to motivate us to do better. In classical Greek, the word referred to any kind of excellence. It could be the excellence of a farmer harvesting his crops, or the excellence of a tool performing well. It speaks of accomplishing that for which the thing was designed or created.

To act in a "praiseworthy" manner means to behave in ways that earn commendation. It describes exemplary actions and admirable behavior worthy of public note.

At the end of this verse, Paul instructs us to think over these things, to meditate on them. He says, "I want you to ponder, to consider. Think about what I've written. Mull it over. See if there's any value in what I'm saying. Take a little time. Don't just listen to it and leave."

In nineteenth-century England, during the great days of revival, after a minister preached, the audience would stay seated and remain for a while to ponder what they'd heard. And what happens in churches today? You'd better not loiter in the center aisle or you'll get run over. By the time the preacher says, "Let us pray," everyone is on their way out.

If you truly want a life yielded to God, you must meditate on the things God instructs you to ponder. Marinate your heart and soul in the eternal message of God's Word. In this way you'll come to the place where you will think and act biblically. And then, finally, you'll start doing that for which you were created.

I love to read Kent Hughes. I've probably sold as many copies of his book, *The Disciplines of a Godly Man*, as any other preacher. Hughes said this about Philippians 4:8: "Each of Paul's ingredients is explicitly positive. The true, the noble, the right, the pure, the lovely, the admirable all defy negative exposition. Each ingredient was, and is, *a matter of personal choice*—and our choices make all the difference in the world."[1]

How you live really is a choice. What will you choose?

A Real Difference for Good

God has good gifts for you, but you have choices to make. You have to desire to do what is right, and then you must become diligent and disciplined and let the Lord reshape your mind.

It won't happen overnight. You didn't get in such poor condition quickly, and you're going to have to give God an opportunity to do His work in you. Then He'll bring you to the place for which He created you.

Don't waste your years. Don't waste your life. Don't be so foolish! The enemy wants to eat the crops that God desires to harvest in your life. You have a choice to make.

Don't allow the devil to corrupt your thinking. Be diligent. Press into Jesus. Get into the Word, and let the Word get into you. Learn to do spiritual battle so you can think biblically. You are not going to act biblically until you start thinking biblically.

Be sure of this: You'll never change the things you're doing until you change the way you think. When you let God change your mind, He'll give you a biblical mind. And then God can use you to begin to make a real difference for good in this world.

3

Dangerous Relationships

Late one evening when I was at home, the phone rang. It turned out to be one of the strangest conversations I've ever had.

I had no idea who would be calling me so late, but I picked up the phone and heard the voice of a woman whom I had never met. But she indicated she knew who I was. Her slurred speech told me that she had been drinking, and her tone of voice told me she had something urgent on her mind.

"Reverend Hunt," she said, "I've been attending First Baptist Church for a while. I really like the church and I'm thinking about joining."

"Well, I hope you do," I replied. "We'd love to have you."

After a time of small talk, she got to the purpose of her call: "Pastor, I have a problem and I need to talk to you about it. I want you to come over to my house so we can talk."

Immediately my defenses went up. I needed more information before I'd even consider meeting with an unknown woman at night.

"Is your husband there?" I asked.

"I'm not married," she answered. "Is that a problem?"

As a matter of fact, it was a *big* problem. I would never meet with a single woman, alone, in her home at night. In all my years of ministry and in all my years of being married, I'd never done that. And I wasn't about to start doing it that night.

"I'm sorry, but I won't be able to do that," I said, trying my best to get the scolding tone out of my voice. "Ma'am, I don't *ever* visit women in their homes when they're by themselves. If you'd like to talk to someone at the church, give us a call in the morning."

Does that seem harsh to you? Do you wonder why I'd refuse to help this woman by taking the time to talk to her in her home? Did I not trust her?

First, I didn't even know her, so I had no reason to trust or distrust her. For all I knew, she had a very real need to talk with someone that night. While I never would have visited her at her home, I did feel compassion for her, and I did pray for her.

Second, I could never honor her request. Visiting a single woman I'd never met, at night, in her home, with no one else there? That would never happen.

Third, I did take into account the matter of trust—but that had far more to do with whether I trusted myself than whether I trusted this strange woman. No, I don't trust myself. While I don't consider sexual temptation a major stronghold in my life, my Bible tells me that "the heart is deceitful above all things, and desperately wicked" (Jeremiah 17:9). That means my heart too.

Because I love my wife and because it sickens me to think of ever doing anything that would hurt her, I must always remain on my guard against any traps the devil might lay for me in *all* areas of sin—even the sins that I doubt tempt me much.

A Matter of Distrust

The apostle Peter wrote some wise words that speak volumes to a man's vulnerability, which includes the possibility of sinning through an inappropriate relationship: "Sanctify the Lord God in your hearts, and always be ready to give a defense to everyone who asks you a reason for the hope that is in you, with meekness and fear" (1 Peter 3:15).

Most of the time when we read this verse, we take it as a command and an encouragement to be ready at all times to share the message of salvation. While it most certainly is talking about that, there's more to it. The verse ends with the word "fear," and according to Greek scholar A.T. Robinson, that word can be rendered "self-distrust."

A man has to understand himself and his sinful nature well enough that he avoids overconfidence in his ability to resist temptation—any kind of temptation. No matter how long we've been walking with Jesus, no matter how strong we may think ourselves to be, every one of us can still give in to temptation, given the right circumstances. We have to know better than to trust ourselves.

In the classic devotional *My Utmost for His Highest*, Oswald Chambers wrote, "Unguarded strength is actually a double weakness, because that is where the least likely temptations will be effective in sapping strength."[2] I love his insight, because it reminds me that no matter how strong I think I am, I still have to guard my heart against both obvious and subtle spiritual dangers.

A Friendly Warning

Dangerous relationships can come in many forms. Adultery may leap to our minds, but many completely nonsexual relationships can send us to the bottom just as quickly. "Do not be deceived," Paul writes, "evil company corrupts good habits" (1 Corinthians 15:33). Does "evil company" sound as generic to you as it does to me?

An unwise business partnership can shipwreck your faith.

A friendship based on some strong appetite could lead to addiction.

Spending too much time with an odd neighbor could cost you your home.

An Internet connection to a faraway "friend" could destroy your family.

Yes, dangerous relationships can be of many types. How many men through the ages have torpedoed their futures and their faith by inviting a stronghold into their lives through some dangerous relationship? I don't know. But you don't have to be one of them.

Paul asks us to note one especially important point about dangerous relationships: They can deceive you. You may think you're going in one direction when in fact you are going in another. Bad company has a strong tendency to corrupt good morals.

Jason Ranew used to work as a prosecuting attorney. He wrote in a blog, "I observed many bright and talented young people as they faced the criminal justice system. Regrettably, their presence in a courtroom almost always came about because of unwise decisions. The collective testimony of these young defendants reveals that long before they were charged with an offense and brought before a judge, they made poor choices of friends."[3]

Did these "bright and talented young people" know where these unwise friendships would take them? No. Were they deceived into forging dangerous relationships that they didn't at first recognize even as shaky, let alone dangerous? Yes.

Ranew painted several quick portraits of some "rising stars" who fell victim to dangerous relationships. None of them saw danger ahead. No doubt they all entered into these new friendships seeing them as exciting, energizing, and a break from the ordinary. I'd like you to hear about two of the young men Ranew eventually saw in court.

> Chuck (names have been changed) was an intelligent high school junior who went to a privileged school and came from a good family. He was athletic, witty and well connected. Although he planned on attending a top university, one day he accepted some less ambitious individuals

into his ever-widening circle of friends. They tempted him to try alcohol and marijuana. Soon he was comfortable with his newfound friends and habits.

One evening, following a day of surfing with his buddies, he went to a party where he drank alcohol and smoked marijuana. He left the party and was arrested for driving under the influence and possession of marijuana. He was convicted of the offenses and spent time in jail. At that point, his life wasn't ruined but his future was certainly tainted. The court made it clear to him that unless he found a new group of friends, this would not be his last visit to the jail cell.

By all accounts, Seth was a good person and a law-abiding citizen, but as a high school senior, he found himself in court on a drug charge. According to what his attorney told me, he wasn't afraid of going to jail for a few days. He feared that merely having a drug conviction on his record would keep him out of a good university and would shatter his dream of becoming an engineer.

I worked with this sincere young man and offered him a deal that did not result in a conviction. Today he is getting ready to enter an engineering program, but if he continues to associate with the same "friends" who helped him get arrested, he might not be in the program long.[4]

As you read these stories of foolish young kids, you may be thinking, *Johnny, Johnny. I appreciate your concern, but I'm not a kid anymore. I know how to choose my friends. Some might be a little rough around the edges, but I'd like to think I can be a good influence on them. None of them are going to get me to choose a life of crime or into drug use. I'm a big boy! I can take care of myself. So relax.*

I hope you're right—I really do. But I know one source that's always right, and that's the Word of God. And listen to what it says about dangerous relationships: "He who walks with wise men will be wise, but the companion of fools will be destroyed" (Proverbs 13:20). Funny thing is, we don't read anything there about big boys or little boys. Instead, it says that *anyone* who hangs around wise individuals will see some of that wisdom rub off on them, and *anyone* who spends a lot of time with fools will end up, well, in the gutter. Big boy or not.

Back to Jason Ranew. He wrote:

> In each of these cases, a decent young person chose to form relationships with foolish and unprincipled individuals. None of [them] appreciated the importance of choosing good friends who would lift them up and make them better persons. Being in a bad circle of friends influenced each of these defendants to abandon good judgment and make choices that led to the courtroom and, in some cases, jail. Beyond the criminal justice system, each person mentioned…is probably scarred for life and may never reach his or her full potential.[5]

Think about what he's saying. He calls Chuck and Seth "decent," not wild or insolent. He says the "foolish and unprincipled individuals" who populated "a bad circle of friends" influenced these "decent" young men "to abandon good judgment and make choices that led to the courtroom and, in some cases, jail." And he says that because of their poor choices, they might already have sacrificed their "full potential."

How does that sad trajectory differ from a "decent" adult who begins to hang around "foolish and unprincipled individuals," men who influence said adult to "abandon good judgment" and make poor choices?

Do you want to be a wise man? Then walk with the wise. Do you crave destruction? Then make fools your companions.

In his best-selling book *Leadership*, Rudy Giuliani, the former mayor of New York, devoted a whole chapter to this issue which he called, "Surround Yourself with Great People." Sounds familiar, doesn't it? I'm certain that leadership guru John Maxwell would agree with both Giuliani and the book of Proverbs. He insists that a leader's potential is determined by those closest to him. John Maxwell calls this "the Law of the Inner Circle"—it's one of what he calls the 21 irrefutable laws of leadership.[6]

May I ask who you are allowing to get closest to you? Do you spend most of your time hanging around people who could be considered wise, or with fools? As you look at your circle of friends, do you see any possible dangerous relationships? Remember, it's easy to get deceived! So don't forget the principle: "Evil company corrupts good habits" (1 Corinthians 15:33).

Regardless of your age or how long you've been a Christian.

Don't Ignore the Stop Signs

Many years ago, well before I started doing men's conferences, I created a bit of a stir among some of the men in the church I served at that time. I had just delivered a sermon about men remaining faithful to their wives and told them, "Guys, you ought never to have lunch with the opposite sex unless your wife or a third party is along—never!"

I thought I'd given the guys some simple, practical wisdom for protecting their marriages and their hearts from any kind of infidelity, whether it included actual sexual sin or not. But a few of the men didn't appreciate what I had to say. After the service, a successful architect who attended the church approached me.

He wasn't smiling.

"I resent what you said this morning," he said, and from the look on his face I could tell he meant it.

"You do?" I answered, genuinely concerned that I might have stepped out of line. "What part of the service offended you?"

"I'm a professional man," he replied. "Sometimes, part of doing business is having lunch with my clients, and sometimes they are female clients. We talk business, and that's it. Nothing more has ever happened, and nothing more ever will happen. I love my wife and kids and I love the Lord. I'm happy with everything I have and I'd never put any of that in jeopardy."

We agreed to disagree on the subject, shook hands, and parted ways for that day. No hard feelings—he didn't leave the church over it, and we remained on friendly terms. But I went home that day wondering if my church considered me some kind of dinosaur preacher, out of touch with the way things really work in the world of modern business.

While I was glad to hear that the architect had a happy marriage and felt no temptation to stray, I continued to stand behind what I said. I still do, even to this day. I've just heard too many stories of heartbreak that started with seemingly innocent meetings between married men and other women.

I think of "Phil," married with two kids. He had a great job working at an accounting firm. He and his wife were reasonably happy with one another and had no major problems in their marriage. It wasn't a perfect union, but Phil felt neither unhappy nor discontented.

One day after work, Phil and several of his co-workers visited the local establishment for happy hour. After everyone had a bite to eat and a drink or two, they departed, leaving Phil and Diane, a thirty-five-year-old married-but-soon-to-be-divorced woman, alone together at the bar. As they started talking, Phil realized that she was charming, funny, and intelligent, and he found himself attracted to her. They had a nice conversation, which included Diane sharing her feelings about her failing marriage. After an hour or so of conversation, Phil and Diane went their separate ways and headed to their respective homes.

Phil had no serious intention of pursuing Diane—but at the same time, he found himself thinking about her almost constantly. He had daydreams about her at work and at home. He even caught himself thinking about her one evening as he and his wife lay in bed, talking about their day.

It's no stretch to say that by not leaving the bar with the rest of his co-workers, Phil put himself in an extremely perilous situation. And though he never acted on his attraction for Diane, he allowed a stronghold to get set up in his mind, one that held him captive for months and one that made life at home very uncomfortable.

Dangerous relationships can happen in any setting—at work, in social settings, even in church—and any man who doesn't purposefully guard himself against inappropriate relationships can end up in a place far worse than where Phil landed.

Dangerous Emotional Bonding

James Dobson taught for years that the number one cause of adulterous relationships was inappropriate emotional bonding, usually as the result of unwise conversations that took place between a married man and "another woman."

Emotional bonding itself is a gift from God. It's a combination of spiritual, emotional, and physical oneness that the Lord gives married couples as they share with one another their spirits, their minds, and their bodies. The problem arises when such bonding occurs between two people not married to one another.

Some things about myself I should never even consider sharing with anyone but Janet. Likewise, there are some things Janet should never share with anyone but me. A married man sometimes runs into trouble when he finds himself sharing intimate information with a woman other than his wife. That's a betrayal of the sanctity of marriage and a betrayal of the woman God gave to him. It's also an effective way to open oneself up to emotional and spiritual strongholds that can damage both the man and his marriage.

Look at it this way: How would you feel if you found out that your wife had been sharing intimate secrets about herself with a man she worked with or knew from church? What if she told him about issues she'd been having in your marriage, topics of discussion that she'd never even talked about with you?

I can't speak for all men, but I'll bet that most of us would feel deeply hurt, angry, and betrayed if our wives were to do that. Not only that, we'd wonder if an affair was about to start…if it hadn't already.

That's just the nature of our relationships with the opposite sex. When a man and a woman start sharing their deepest, most personal secrets and desires with one another, the conversation leads to communion. From there, it's just a short step or two before the communion leads to consummation.

When this process takes place between a married man and a woman other than his wife, it brings very serious consequences. That is why we need to be always on our guard and why we need a plan of action to avoid such dangerous relationships. No man needs this kind of stronghold in his life.

Protecting Yourself from the Hazards

Years ago, David Frost interviewed the great evangelist Billy Graham. During their conversation, Frost asked Billy how he had remained faithful to Ruth Graham, at that time his wife of sixty-four years. Mr. Graham answered that he had made a commitment long ago to never be with someone of the opposite sex by himself—never in a car, never in a restaurant, anywhere.

Billy later explained that his decision never to visit with, travel with, or eat meals alone with a woman other than his wife wasn't just to protect his marriage, but also to avoid the appearance of any kind of inappropriate relationship. Mr. Graham was protecting his marriage, yes, but he was also protecting the amazing evangelistic ministry God had given him.

Billy Graham faced a lot of criticism for what became known as "the Graham Rule," mainly from those who believe that it hurts a godly woman's chances of becoming more deeply involved in church ministries. I acknowledge these criticisms, but I've also seen the devastation caused when married men fail to exercise wisdom and caution in how they relate to women other than their wives. I've seen the heartbreak men have caused themselves and their families when they entered into relationships that may have started out relatively innocently, but end up becoming something they never thought could happen.

Run Away

During a recent conversation with a friend, the two of us made tentative plans to get together later. I told him I wasn't sure of my schedule over the next few weeks and asked him to shoot me an email so we could firm up our plans. His reply startled me.

"I don't have a computer," he said.

He doesn't have a computer? I thought. *Who in the world doesn't have a computer in this day and age?*

"I don't even use a computer," he added, and then he explained his reason. "I used to have a computer, but I got hooked on Internet pornography. I couldn't break free of it, so I decided to get rid of my computer."

"Well, God bless you," I said, and then asked him to call me instead of emailing me.

Our conversation reminded me of the words of Jesus: "If your right eye causes you to sin, pluck it out and cast it from you; for it is more profitable for you that one of your members perish, than for your whole body to be cast into hell" (Matthew 18:9).

Getting rid of that computer was a practical application of some radical biblical teaching. This dear brother in the Lord took Jesus' warnings about the perils of sin seriously, and he took some decisive action by casting away the offending member—his computer.

Avoiding the stronghold of a dangerous relationship, whatever that relationship might be, sometimes means simply getting away from it. That is the message behind these words from the wise King Solomon: "Do not enter the path of the wicked, and do not walk in the way of evil. Avoid it, do not travel on it; turn away from it and pass on" (Proverbs 4:14-15).

A friend of mine, "Bill," had worked for himself for many years. He liked the self-employed life, but if you know that world at all, you recognize that it can have a lot of ups and downs. Business and clients come and go, checks get sent late or not at all. In one of the down times, Bill got an offer from a reputable company to join its staff. He had some misgivings about the company's president, but he shoved them aside because he thought the man had probably changed since the two had interacted a few years before.

Bill joined the company and within a few weeks the president asked him to join him on a business trip to Southern California to visit some prospective clients. Bill happily complied and thought, *Great! This will give me a chance to lay to rest my lingering doubts.*

It didn't turn out quite that way.

As the trip progressed, Bill grew increasingly uneasy with the president's style of doing business. While the man never did or suggested anything overtly illegal or unethical, Bill felt that, as a rule of thumb, his boss seemed to inch as close to the line as possible. The whole trip made Bill feel uncomfortable and unsettled.

When he returned home, Bill had some decisions to make. He could always return to his freelance business, but he really liked the financial stability of working within a larger company. He also loved most of his new colleagues. If they didn't sense a problem with the president, then why should he let his concerns trouble him so much?

Within a few weeks, Bill knew what he had to do. He couldn't shake his apprehensions about his boss, regardless of what his colleagues might think. He realized he might be wrong about the man, but he recognized that even his lingering suspicions would negatively affect his job performance. He therefore regretfully turned in his resignation and returned to the up-and-down professional world he'd known before. He did so because, right or wrong, he saw his relationship with his boss as dangerous. He didn't want to adopt the methods he'd observed on the business trip in Southern California, and he thought that if he stayed with the company, he might well be pressed into doing just that. So he said, "Good-bye."

A while back, someone outlined for me a great strategy for avoiding the kind of temptation a dangerous relationship can present: "Johnny," he said, "I just want to remind you that you can't coast for even one day. You've got to keep running."

I know that even at my age, if I stop running from what I perceive as dangerous relationships, I'll end up in the wrong place. The same thing is true for you. If you don't run when you should, someday you'll turn around and notice a chain link fence surrounding a massive building going up on your property. As you look around, you'll see a big sign posted at the gate: *Stronghold Under Construction. Just Step Away, Fool.*

Wisdom for the Battle

No man in his right mind intentionally sets out to build a stronghold that takes him prisoner and keeps him locked up for years behind iron bars. I think that's why the devil so craftily uses what seems like a harmless, maybe even helpful, relationship to build that stronghold.

- Don't fall for his tactics.
- Don't trust yourself.

- Don't choose foolish and unprincipled friends.

- Don't ignore the stop signs.

- Don't bond emotionally where you shouldn't.

- Don't fail to exercise caution.

- Don't be afraid to run away.

But do hang out with the wise—and let their wisdom arm you against all kinds of dangerous relationships.

4

The Distraction of Attraction

I have a friend who once needed to attend an important meeting about twenty miles north of where he'd been staying. On the day of the meeting, he pulled out of the driveway as usual and got on the onramp to the Interstate. As he drove, he got distracted by all sorts of things: unfamiliar wildlife, beautiful terrain, even his own thoughts. At one point he thought, *It seems like it's taking a long time to get there today.* But he dismissed the thought and drove on.

About five minutes later, he knew he was in trouble. A little road sign told him that in two miles he'd arrive in a nice little town *about sixty miles south of where he needed to be.*

My friend had driven forty miles, about twice as far as he needed to go, in the exact opposite direction. And he never even knew it until he saw the little sign. He immediately turned around, sped up the highway, and arrived for the last few minutes of his meeting.

That's bad enough, but imagine what might have happened had he decided on his way south to stop at some picturesque spot to snap a few pictures. Suppose the view had so captivated him that he spent a couple of hours photographing the deer, the flowers, the trees, the lush hills, the vault of the clear, blue sky. By the time he looked at his watch, he would have missed the meeting entirely. And since he wouldn't yet have realized that he had traveled in the wrong direction, he would have wasted more time rushing south when he should have gone north. Maybe by that point he would have felt so preoccupied that he would've missed the sign. Next stop, Antarctica!

Our world dangles all kinds of distractions in front of our faces. Often those momentary distractions lead to attractions that capture our long-term interest, frequently to our detriment.

Do you know that the very same thing can happen in our spiritual lives? Distractions have a way of leading to attractions that end up breaking ground for a stronghold.

Distractions, Distractions

If you were to look up the word *distraction* in a dictionary or study it on the web, you would discover that the term refers to a passive phenomenon. You can get distracted and not even know it. You might not even be thinking about anything in particular, and suddenly this unexpected something comes into view and snatches your attention. That's why it's so dangerous.

Amanda Kloehr knows about distractions. In 2008 she got in her car, buckled her seat belt, and started driving. Somewhere along the way, she got distracted. "It's not like she was doing anything horrible," reported one story; "she hadn't been drinking or doing drugs before driving, she was wearing her seat-belt. She was just distracted—maybe checking her messages or texting on her phone, or maybe finding a good song on the radio or checking out where she was going on her GPS—she doesn't really remember which. All she knows is that this preoccupation, not keeping her full attention on her driving, put her and everyone else driving around her at risk. And, she paid a heavy price for this."[7]

A collision with a tractor trailer left Amanda's car mangled and buried in wreckage. An emergency responder with twenty years of experience assumed nobody could have survived such a horrific wreck, but then he heard Amanda's screams. Amanda lived, but "after many surgeries, facial reconstruction and the loss of an eye, she still considers herself lucky she survived and didn't kill anyone else."[8]

Distracted drivers kill thousands of men and women each year in the United States and injure far more. "We are so used to instant information," wrote the article's author. "We can't wait to find the latest news, update a status, friend someone on Facebook. But, is it really that important? Of course not—but it's a mindset we are going to have to change if safer driving is going to be made a higher priority in our society. The cost is just too high if we don't."[9]

Distraction can come with a high cost, whether in our daily lives or our spiritual lives. Distraction speaks of dividing one's attention or of a thing that prevents concentration. Sometimes it amuses or entertains and ends up diverting our focus. Originally the word meant "mental disturbance." The term speaks of a riot, a tumult.

Distraction is a state of mind in which one's attention gets diverted—and we're living in days when we face countless mental distractions. In every sermon I've ever written, I've put great detail in writing the first three sentences. That way, I know I'll have my audience for the first minute. After that, many will get diverted from paying attention.

Have you ever heard someone say, "The Christian life just isn't what it used to be for me"? Maybe that's you. Could it be that *you've* changed, that *you've* moved? Maybe you've become distracted. Could it be that something else is pulling you away, something that you didn't even see coming? Confusion, disorder, frenzy, interruptions, preoccupation, beguilement—all of that fits into the idea of distraction. Distraction implies a side entrance. Even when men are "there" for the important things, distractions redirect their attention to other stuff.

May I ask you a question? What are the distractions in your life?

Because distractions are passive, you probably feel you have them under control. You vaguely realize they are there and you know enough to beware of them. But let me assure you, distractions are doing more of a number on you than you know. If you'll get honest with God about them, the Lord will help you to protect yourself.

Distractions are nothing new, of course. The apostle Paul once advised his Corinthian friends against beginning some romantic relationships that might cause them real problems due to some political or cultural trouble at that time. "This I say for your own profit, not that I may put a leash on you, but for what is proper," he wrote, "and that you may serve the Lord without distraction" (1 Corinthians 7:35).

With a thousand distractions vying for your attention all the time, why add more if you can avoid them? One of the best ways to prevent strongholds from ever getting built is to serve the Lord without distraction. So why not get rid of as many distractions as possible?

From Distraction to Attraction

While distractions differ from attractions, the former often leads to the latter. First, let's consider how the two compare with one another.

Distractions	**Attractions**
Passive	Active
Unplanned	Planned
Breaks concentration	Redirects concentration
Often unfamiliar	Always familiar
Momentary	Long-term
Curiosity piqued	Appetite indulged

Unlike distraction, attraction is active. It refers to something you already have an interest in, something that has previously captured your attention. Therefore you seek it out. You think about it even when you're not actively engaged with it. The synonyms for *attraction* include to allure, to appeal, to bait, captivate, charm, draw, entice, invite, seduce, solicit, tempt. Attraction speaks of an active motion toward something that already has captured your interest.

While all of us feel attracted to any number of things, and many of them are good and natural, problems arise when we indulge the attractions that hurt our souls, injure our families, and harm our relationship with God. And some attractions can kill.

Blogger Jim Goad reports, "Late in 2013 professional truck driver Jorge Espinoza was blithely hurtling down the road at 65 MPH with his giant steel death machine set on cruise control as he was 'looking at pictures of women on Facebook.' According to police reports, he had been perusing 'photographs of several women in provocative positions, wearing little clothing,' and 'photographs of a woman in a low cut dress' when he should have been looking at the road. As a result, he smashed into five police vehicles, killing one officer."[10]

Many men make fun of reports like this, I know. I'm guessing a Texan named Chance Bothe used to be one of them. Goad wrote that in January of 2012, Bothe "was driving his pickup truck and texting back and forth with a friend. He texted, 'I need to quit texting, because I could die in a car accident,' then accidentally drove his truck off a cliff. He survived, but only after suffering a 'broken neck, a crushed face, a fractured skull, and traumatic brain injuries.'"[11]

In my several decades as a pastor, I've seen all kinds of attractions destroy the faith of good men. Whenever an attraction becomes a stronghold, tragedy inevitably follows. If I had to rank the ten attractions that ruin men most, my list would look something like this:

Attractions that Often Become Strongholds

1. Bigger career
2. Greener grass
3. Specific personal weakness
4. Money
5. Pride
6. Power
7. Sex
8. Corporate clout
9. Titles
10. Notoriety

This isn't an exhaustive list, nor is it a scientific one. The truth is, many attractions in our world have the capacity to divert us from living as fully devoted followers of Christ. Whenever we latch on to those attractions, we build strongholds and so fail to become God's men. Most of the time, our own self-indulgence leads us to permit some attraction to divert us from pure devotion to Christ. We really believe we will enjoy this attraction more than we will enjoy our fellowship with Jesus. Listen to what James said: "Each one is tempted when he's drawn away by his own desires and is enticed" (James 1:14). He uses a word for "baiting the hook."

I'll be frank with you. If every man who has his name on the roll at Woodstock—every man who at one time said this ministry meant enough to him that he publicly joined our church—showed up one Sunday morning, we would have to rent the arena downtown. We couldn't cram all of them into our buildings. Some attraction or other has pulled all these guys away.

What attractions are trying to pull you away?

We live in an era of entitlement and self-centeredness. Many of us have so fallen in love with the philosophy of this world that the prevailing culture has influenced us more than we are influencing and confronting the culture. As a result, we have forged a friendship with the world—and that's become a real problem. It's a variety of distractions and attractions that have seriously hurt us and our walk with Christ. So what's the answer?

A Slave of Christ

If you ask the Bible to name the traits of a godly person, it will give you two primary characteristics. If you have a genuine desire to be a godly man, the Bible tells you both what you won't do and what you will do:

1. You won't present the members of your body as slaves of unrighteousness.

2. You will present the members of your body as slaves of Christ.

When the apostle Paul tells you to avoid presenting "your members as slaves of uncleanness and of lawlessness, leading to more lawlessness," he means that once sin gets hold of you, it will never be satisfied with the amount of you it has. Ephesians 4:22 uses a progressive present tense verb to instruct you to "put off, concerning your former conduct, the old man, which grows corrupt." Sin is *always* progressive. Sin is never satisfied where it is.

I once led a men's conference in Stark, Florida. Stark is famous for just one thing: its large prison. That's where serial killer Ted Bundy was incarcerated. James Dobson went to Stark to speak with Bundy and videotape his testimony. He wanted to show America how men could be set free from the depravity that had destroyed Bundy.

Bundy explained that he started out with what he called soft porn. Soon he got even more out of control. He progressed to hardcore pornography, and then he was no longer satisfied with that. He went on to pornography that depicted violence and murder, and then he wanted to act out what he saw. He began to have sex with women, then kill them, cut their bodies into pieces, and bury them. He confessed to killing some thirty young women, but some believe he may have murdered as many as a hundred individuals, both women and men.

I was in town in January 1989, the day he was electrocuted. Signs popped up in front of the convenience stores and fast food places, all of them saying variations of the same basic message: "Turn your lights off at six so we can give him a greater charge."

Bundy went much further than the average man, but the stronghold that got him is the same one that's ruining marriages and men and ministries across America. Sin is always progressive. It always wants more of you than it has, and it won't be satisfied until it has destroyed all of you.

We'd better wake up! The latest research is nearly unbelievable. Did you know that 79 percent of men ages 18 to 30 view porn at least once a month?[12] Viewing pornography has become socially acceptable. Teens think of it as a huge attraction—and it keeps them from becoming fully devoted followers of Christ.

Lawlessness, regardless of its kind or stripe, always leads to more lawlessness. Sin is never satisfied. It always wants to take more. That's what drugs do. That's what alcohol does. That's what gambling does. That's the normal, natural progression.

And only when we become eager slaves of Christ—only when we willingly submit the members of our body to His lordship—will we win this battle. Only then will we tear down the strongholds that threaten to annihilate us.

Are You a Role Model?

I want to be so committed to Jesus that, by the power of Christ, I can be a godly role model. Paul told his friends in Philippi, "The things you learned from me"—the things you received, you heard, and you saw me do—"imitate those things" (Philippians 4:9). Don't forget that the apostle insisted he had clay feet, just like the rest of us. He saw nothing good in himself, nothing good in his flesh. And yet he told his Christian friends that, by that point in his life, God had so worked in his thinking processes that he lived out the Lord's principles. So he told them, "What you saw me do, imitate. Follow me as I follow Christ" (see 1 Corinthians 4:16; 11:1; 2 Thessalonians 3:7).

In Jesus' name, we ought to be able to say to our sons and

daughters, "If you want to know how to live, pray for me, because I want you to see in me and learn from me and hear from me how to live this life in Jesus." This is not Pastor Johnny's thoughts or a specific denomination's way. This is God's way. All Christian men should be able to say, "Emulate what you see in me. Whatever you see Dad do, imitate."

We may have to go to our kids and acknowledge when we've blown it. When they hear us say unkind things to our spouse, for example, we need to say to them, "Hey kids, I want you to hear right in front of your mom that I shouldn't have said what I said to her. I've asked God to forgive me, and I've asked your mother to forgive me. And kids, I would appreciate your forgiveness too, because I want to model a life that truly honors almighty God." It takes a real man's man to do that.

From Glory to Glory

God wants to take you from glory to glory. When you make a commitment to Jesus Christ, He is not satisfied with your commitment until He has all of you. This is where we often miss the target.

We get one area of our life cleaned up, and when God speaks to us about another area, we don't respond. We say, "I don't need to respond. I already responded last night." But He dealt with you last night about *that*. Right now He's dealing with you about *this*.

"If that's true," you say, "then why doesn't He just show everything I need to change all at once?"

I'll tell you why. He refrains because He's gracious. On one occasion Jesus told His disciples, "I still have many things to say to you, but you cannot bear *them* now" (John 16:12). If Jesus emptied the whole dump truck at once, it would overwhelm us. We're just too immature, too ignorant, too wicked.

When it comes to dealing with our sins, a big part of our problem is that we have the attitude "I'm a good person. I'm not Ted Bundy. I'm not as bad as he was." But the Bible says no good thing dwells in our flesh (see Romans 7:18). It says there is no one who is righteous (Romans 3:10-11). Not a single person! And the Bible doesn't say merely that our hearts are wicked; it calls our hearts "*desperately wicked*" (Jeremiah 17:9). Until we understand that and believe it, we'll never have any success in knocking down the strongholds the enemy has erected in our lives.

God wants you to come to the end of yourself, to recognize that He's your only hope. Struggling more isn't going to get you over the top. You can't succeed that way, no matter how much you struggle. Paul wrote, "So now present your members as slaves of righteousness for holiness" (Romans 6:19).

I'm passionate about this subject because I'm writing out of my own experience. Some years ago, I got distracted and veered from the path God had put me on. I stopped listening to Him as I should and started doing my own thing in ministry. It cost me dearly. I'm writing now out of my own journey, out of my experience of what Jesus, in grace, did in my heart. I learned that I, like everyone else, have to repeatedly focus on three key things:

1. **Renew my faith.** Yesterday's faith doesn't cut it for today's challenges.

2. **Reclaim God's promises.** All of God's promises are *yes* in Christ, but we have to continually draw on them and bank on them to overcome the new hurdles we face.

3. **Resolve to correct unhealthy habits and build new ones.** Habits grow gradually, so slowly that often we don't see them developing. When a crisis hits, these habits get revealed for what they are, whether unhealthy or helpful. Then the task is to dismantle the destructive ones and build the useful ones. That requires both getting the wrong out *and* getting the right in.

My friend Dr. John Edmund Haggai is the ninety-two-year-old founder and CEO of the Haggai Institute. He's a great missiologist with a superb mind. Each month he sends me some study notes. During the dark time when I struggled in ministry, he sent me the following note: "An idol is anyone or anything that has a greater formative influence in your life than God." I needed that reminder.

We have to be so careful! Distractions can easily lead to attractions that cause us to veer off course. And before we know it, we find ourselves in a place we never wanted to be. When anything in your life becomes a constant rival for your devotion to Jesus Christ, you'd better be careful. It may be an idol worming its way into your world. Before too long, you won't be able to remember the last time you had true and enduring fellowship with Jesus. The money you used to give to support God's kingdom now supports your idol. Anything or anyone that has gained more and greater formative influence in your life than Christ is a gift from hell.

A Jealous God

Did you know that God calls Himself a "jealous" God (Exodus 20:5; 34:14)? By this He means, "I'm not satisfied to have just a part of you."

Why should we expect anything else? No married man says, "I don't mind if my wife flirts around. If I'm busy this week, hey, maybe somebody else can take her to dinner." That just doesn't happen. And the Lord says to you, "That's how I feel about you. But there are distractions in your life that have turned into attractions, and they are keeping you from Me. You no longer have time for even a quick devotion."

God is saying, "I want the best of you. In fact, I want *all* of you."

James put a sharp point on this truth when he wrote—to *Christians*: "Adulterers and adulteresses! Do you not know that friendship with the world is enmity with God? Whoever therefore wants to be a friend of the world makes himself an enemy of God. Or do you think that the Scripture says in vain, 'The Spirit who dwells in us yearns jealously'?" (James 4:4-5).

Those who want to be a friend of the world, James insists, have chosen that relationship over being God's friend. He sees no possibility of a balancing act here, no spinning of two plates so that someone can do both well. No, it's an either/or choice. Those who choose friendship with the world have crossed the line, even if they still show up in church.

And notice James doesn't say that *God* makes these men into enemies. Rather, such a man "*makes himself* an enemy of God." That indicates a conscious intent. That man chooses to make himself an enemy of God. The Lord has never been fond of religious balancing acts.

Not long after the Lord destroyed idolatrous Israel and sent her into Assyrian captivity, some of the poor people left behind intermingled with foreign settlers. These people "worshiped the LORD, but they also served their own gods in accordance with the customs of the nations from which they had been brought" (2 Kings 17:33 NIV). In fact, "even while these people were worshiping the LORD, they were serving their idols" (2 Kings 17:41 NIV). Eventually God destroyed them all.

God doesn't want just a part of you. He insists on having all of you. He wants to bless you in every way possible—and He can't do that unless He has all of you.

Needed: Continuous Conversion

Some men are committed just enough to be miserable. I believe the most miserable man in the body of Christ is the one who has been unwilling to say, "Lord, take all the territory of my heart. I want to be a fully devoted follower of Jesus Christ."

Oswald Chambers wrote, "We have to be continually converted all the days of our lives, continually to turn to God as children. If we trust to our wits instead of God, we produce consequences for which God will hold us responsible...The relation of the natural to the spiritual is one of continuous conversion and it is the one thing we object to. There are whole tracks of our life which have not been brought into subjection and it can be done only by His continuous conversion."[13]

Chambers did not mean that we need to get saved all over again. He insisted, rather, that we must make a fresh, new commitment—a continual renewing of our faith to almighty God. He wrote, "Slowly but surely we can claim the whole territory for the Spirit of God."[14]

No distraction has to keep you from God's best. No attraction has to lead to a stronghold that ruins your life. *You* can claim the whole territory—all of it—for the Spirit of God. And what will God do with all that territory? Who knows? But if what He's done in the past is any indication, it promises to be spectacular.

5

The Rationalization of Temptation

There is a statement that summarizes, for me, one of the biggest problems of today's church, and one of the biggest reasons so many of us struggle with strongholds.

Can you guess it? Here's the statement: "Well, no one is perfect."

The problem is we use that excuse to rationalize the sin in our lives. We use it to say, "Yes, I'm giving in to defeat in that one area. But that's not so bad, because I have victory in another."

I can't tell you how many times I've heard men offer that excuse, or a variation of it, for their sinful behavior. Take a look at some of the following rationalizations and see if you haven't heard them from the mouths of your own brothers in Christ. Maybe you've even thought them or spoken them yourself:

> "God wants me to be happy, and I know I'll be happier with this new woman than I am with my wife."
>
> "Everybody sins, so what's the big deal?"
>
> "I just love her so much, and there's so much passion between us."

"I came from a family of alcoholics, so I think God understands when I have too much to drink."

"Everybody else is doing it, so why shouldn't I?"

Adrian Rogers taught me to think of my life as a hundred-acre field. All the devil wants is one acre, while he lets you have the other ninety-nine. He's okay with letting you control almost all of it. "But," Adrian said, "anytime you give the devil one acre, he'll take it right in the heart of your land. And that gives him access in and out of *all* of your property. He won't be satisfied until he takes it all."

You and I give the devil his one acre whenever we live by the statement, "Well, no one is perfect." That's all the devil needs from us. He'll take that one acre and use it to gain control of the other ninety-nine.

Don't Blame Me

Any of us can easily slide into blaming our circumstances for our sin, whether it be our dysfunctional upbringing, our current family situation, or our financial difficulties. Such blame-shifting is as old as time. Starting with Adam, men have been doing it almost since the very beginning.

Take a look at the third chapter of Genesis. God had given Adam a perfect garden to live in and the perfect mate to help him care for it. But the pair did the one thing God had commanded them not to do. When they sinned, Adam felt something God had never intended for His prized creation to feel: shame.

When God confronted Adam over his sinful choice, the man didn't confess. Neither did he seek God's forgiveness. Instead, he blamed Eve. Listen to Adam's rationalization: "The woman whom *You gave to be with me*, she gave me of the tree, and I ate" (Genesis 3:12).

Rather than willingly confess that he had chosen to disobey God, Adam told his Creator that Eve had pushed him into sin. And because God had given him Eve as his wife, God Himself was also to blame.

Blaming...God?

I wish I were kidding when I say I've heard men try to excuse their sexual sin by claiming they had such strong inner passions and appetites that they had no choice but to indulge them. "I'm just oversexed," they'll say. "Something about the way I'm wired makes it impossible for me to resist sex. I just *have* to have it."

Such lame excuses reveal what I consider an evil, twisted rationalization: "God made me this way."

This may shock you, but multitudes of Christian men believe that because God is sovereign and therefore is ultimately in control of everything, then somehow He has preordained that His people give in to sin, at least occasionally. It's a delusion especially common among those who struggle with some specific sin. But it's a deception straight from Satan himself.

Know this: God *never* ordains sin, and He *never* approves of it. Yes, He absolutely knows that we all have a bent toward sin and evil, and He knows that we're going to stumble and fall from time to time. But it is absolutely wrong to believe or to say that God desires anything for His people but that they live in victory over sin.

The apostle James addressed this rationalization very directly when he wrote, "Let no one say when he is tempted, 'I am tempted by God'; for God cannot be tempted by evil, nor does He Himself tempt anyone" (James 1:13).

In essence, James is telling Christians to stop making excuses for their sin, and to never, *ever* excuse their wrongdoing by suggesting that God had anything to do with the temptation. Writing under the inspiration of God's Holy Spirit, James warned all men to steer clear of their bent toward rationalization. He said, "Stop trying to shift the blame for your sin away from yourself. *You* chose to indulge. Now own up to it."

No Christian should ever imagine that God would ever, directly or indirectly, tempt them to commit sin or do evil. God cannot tempt men to sin because it violates His sinless nature. God can never tempt us to sin, nor can anyone or anything tempt Him to sin.

So where does temptation really originate? What is its source? James doesn't leave us in suspense: "Each one is tempted when he is drawn away by his own desires and enticed. Then, when desire has conceived, it gives birth to sin; and sin, when it is full-grown, brings forth death" (James 1:14-15).

That really puts the responsibility where it belongs, doesn't it? James has already told us that temptation never comes from God. Now he claims it doesn't come primarily from the devil, either, although our enemy works overtime trying to get us to sin. In fact, the inclination to give in to temptation originates with the evil desires and sinful cravings dwelling within each of us. Sure, the devil knows how to put temptation in our path (he even tried it with Jesus); but the tendency to cave into temptation has its roots within every man's own fallen heart.

If you're trying to rationalize or make excuses for your sin, or trying to shift the blame for it to others, including God, you need to back up. God has stated in His Word that His ultimate purpose for you is your complete holiness and perfection. Paul made this point beautifully when he wrote, "Whom He foreknew, He also predestined to be conformed to the image of His Son" (Romans 8:29).

Christlikeness is God's goal for each of us. It is God's will for each believing man to be conformed to the image of His dear, spotless Son.

You will never have victory over temptation until you stop making excuses for yourself and instead take full responsibility for your sinful decisions. When you do wrong, you *choose* to do wrong. And when you choose to do wrong, you give the devil the real estate he needs to set up strongholds behind your defenses.

Temptation: No One Is Immune

Have you ever struggled with a troublesome, persistent sin in your life but felt afraid to talk to your brothers in Christ about it? You feared they might look down on you or judge you.

I've learned a few things about confession over the years, and one of them is that none of us faces any temptation that millions of other men haven't already faced. That's why we often get a certain response when we talk to a Christian brother about what we imagine to be our own unique set of temptations: "You too?" As Solomon wrote, "There is nothing new under the sun" (Ecclesiastes 1:9).

Satan wants you to think, *I'm struggling with this, but I can't tell my brother about it. He just wouldn't understand.* You need to counter his lie with the truth: "No temptation has overtaken you except such as is common to man; but God is faithful, who will not allow you to be tempted beyond what you are able, but with the temptation will also make the way of escape, that you may be able to bear it" (1 Corinthians 10:13).

This side of eternity, we can't escape the temptation to sin. It's a terrible but unavoidable fact of life. No Christian has ever been free of solicitations to do evil. We live in a fallen, sinful world (I sometimes call it Temptation Island), and that world is filled with all kinds of potholes of temptation. The devil is an expert at nudging us toward those potholes. When we fall in, however, we're the ones responsible for making the choice to fall.

Those who don't know Jesus Christ are tempted to sin too, of course, and they give in to temptation with great regularity. What else would we expect? Sinners sin. But we who walk with Jesus, especially when we desire to make our lives a brilliant testimony to the grace and goodness of God, *will* be tempted to sin.

Do you have eyes and ears? Then you know temptation is an unfortunate part of the human experience. Even God's own Son, Jesus Christ, who is 100 percent God and 100 percent human, did not escape temptation. Temptation comes to every man.

At the beginning of Jesus' earthly ministry, the Spirit led Him "into the wilderness to be tempted by the devil" (Matthew 4:1). Notice that the passage doesn't say that the Spirit led Jesus into the wilderness so the devil could *try* to tempt Him. No, the temptation was both real and potent. The man Jesus had a divine appointment with the devil in order to be legitimately tempted.

The Bible declares that Jesus was "in all points tempted as we are, yet without sin" (Hebrews 4:15). And how did Jesus manage to rebuff the devil's temptations? For one thing, He knew exactly what the enemy had in mind for Him. But even more, He had determined to depend completely upon His Father in heaven for the strength and focus He needed to complete His earthly mission.

I pray this regularly: "Help me, God, in the name of Jesus, to never become desensitized to sin. Remind me daily to remember that I have a spiritual enemy who wants more than anything to tempt me into sinning and thereby dishonor You and bring reproach on myself as one of Your children."

I also ask God to never let me forget what and who I really am… and what I'm capable of if I don't walk closely with Him.

You Have to Know Yourself

The Bible gives many names to the devil. It calls him a liar, a murderer, a thief…the list goes on. In 1 Thessalonians 3:5, Paul called Satan "the tempter," which he most certainly is. The devil works 24/7 to tempt us to do evil, because he knows that if he can get us to sin, he can rob us of our joy, our fellowship with God, even our very souls. He also knows that getting us to sin gives him the opportunity to set up powerful strongholds in our lives so that he can continue his attacks from a position of greater strength. This is why the apostle Peter warns us, "Be sober, be vigilant; because your adversary the devil walks about like a roaring lion, seeking whom he may devour" (1 Peter 5:8).

Your adversary wants to destroy your soul. He knows your weaknesses. He knows that even though you desire to live a godly life, you're still a fallen, sinful human being with a lot of ugliness inside you.

Paul, a man who dedicated himself to preaching the message of salvation through Jesus Christ, understood this well. "I know that in me (that is, in my flesh) nothing good dwells," he wrote, "for to will is present with me, but how to perform what is good I do not find" (Romans 7:18).

What a great godly truth for those of us who find it easy to rationalize and make excuses for our sinful attitudes and behaviors! Paul made no excuses for himself. He didn't try to rationalize or shift the blame for his sinful choices. He had the humility to admit that nothing good dwelled inside him, apart from what Christ was doing.

I grasp only too well what Paul meant about the depravity of his flesh. Like Paul, I know that my own heart brims with all kinds of sin and wickedness. I know that, apart from Christ, sin would rule me with a rod of iron and pave my path to an eternity in hell. How do I know this? Jesus has told me so.

Jesus flat-out declared, "For from within, out of the heart of men, proceed evil thoughts, adulteries, fornications, murders, thefts, covetousness, wickedness, deceit, lewdness, an evil eye, blasphemy, pride, foolishness. All these evil things come from within and defile a man" (Mark 7:20-23).

I see Jesus' words as more than a mere laundry list of the evil that lies within fallen human hearts. In these words, I hear Jesus telling me, "Johnny, this is an inventory of what's inside *you*. It's the sin you are a millisecond away from falling into if you don't yield yourself to Me every moment of your life."

I don't take pleasure in thinking about what I'm capable of doing when I fail to remain vigilant, when I stop yielding to and depending upon Jesus. But I like even less the idea of giving the enemy of my soul a stronghold in my life. That's why I have to continually remind myself that apart from Jesus Christ, I'm capable of committing every sin on Jesus' list.

What a humbling thought! You and I need to do everything we can to leave no room in our hearts for rationalizing or blame-shifting. Oh, how vulnerable we all are to giving in to temptation! Our sinful natures naturally gravitate toward sin.

How crucially important it is to remind ourselves, on a frequent basis, of the true nature of sin and temptation.

The Devil's Tackle Box

Anyone who's been into fishing for the past three decades probably remembers the television show *Fishin' with Orlando Wilson*, which aired on WTBS and The Nashville Network in the 1980s and 1990s.

I had the privilege of leading Orlando, a good friend, to faith in Jesus Christ. In return, he taught me a lot about fishing. He's one of those guys who always seems to catch fish, no matter how picky the slimy creatures are and no matter how bad the conditions become on the water.

One thing that makes Orlando such a great angler is that he knows when to change the bait he's using. When the fish show no interest in crankbaits, he switches to the spinnerbaits. If the spinnerbaits don't work, he tries the jigs or topwater plugs. More often than not (*far* more often), Orlando figures out what looks good to the fish on any given day. When that happens, he puts a lot of fish in the boat.

Any successful fisherman knows that fish, by their nature, are drawn to things they see as good to eat. He also knows that what fish find irresistible can change due to a variety of circumstances— water and weather conditions, the time of year, and so forth. An expert fisherman knows how to work around those circumstances and present a bait or a lure that looks good and smells good to the fish he wants to catch. When he finds something that appeals to the fish's senses, the animal loses all caution and grabs something not good for it. It gets itself hooked. And then it's too late.

It's the same way with people.

We've all heard that old line from 1960s comic Flip Wilson: "The devil made me do it!" A lot of Christian men make that excuse when they sin. Rather than take responsibility for their rebellious actions, they rationalize that the devil put too big a temptation in front of them to resist.

The truth is, of course, the devil can't *make* us do anything. While he's a powerful, crafty enemy, he has his limitations. He can, however, put all manner of temptations in front of us. If a certain bait doesn't work, he'll try another. With thousands of years of practice, he's become an expert fisherman. Still, he can't *make* us chomp down on any of his enticing lures. We choose whether we bite or pass.

In some ways, the devil knows us better than we know ourselves. He knows that a lure that might work under one situation, or for one man, might not work for another (at least on any given day). But he has a tackle box filled with thousands of beautiful, shiny baits, and he knows which ones to use to draw us out and entice us to lose all caution. If greed and materialism don't work, then he'll try self-sufficiency and pride. And if self-sufficiency and pride don't do the trick, he'll opt for a smorgasbord of sexual sins. And if that fails, he has an unlimited supply of more exotic or more specialized baits.

The devil throws these temptations at us with the goal of getting us to rationalize some choice to sin, of getting us to believe that one little sin can't hurt. And when he finally gets us to bite, he has us hooked. What was once a temptation becomes a sin, and before long what was a sin becomes a stronghold. And at that point, he's basically neutralized us. Until we raze the stronghold, we present no threat to any of his offensives.

The devil is never satisfied with just making us stumble and fall into one sin. He intends to set up strongholds in our lives—the more the better. And he gets the process started by luring us into taking just one tiny bite of just one little lure.

Without Christ empowering and enabling us, we have no power against the devil's temptations. We're as helpless as a hungry bass staring up at what he believes is a tasty little minnow, but which in reality is an invitation to become a fisherman's dinner.

As powerless as we are, however, we still have an advantage—one that the devil has no power to overcome.

Depend on God

A few years back, I traveled with some of my staff to Budapest, Hungary. After a nice dinner at an American-style restaurant, we made our way back to our hotel rooms. The hotel was within easy walking distance of the restaurant, and my staff members left for the hotel before I did.

Several minutes into my stroll back to my room, I passed a group of provocatively dressed young women. *Prostitutes*, I immediately thought. I hoped against all hope that the young women wouldn't see me, but they did.

I was in for a real-life picture of how temptation works.

One of the young women locked her eyes on me, smiled broadly, and greeted me with an overly friendly, "Hello! How are you?" I wanted more than anything to flee the scene, so I kept walking but answered politely, "Great! How are you all?"

Immediately the conversation, if you could call it that, turned into something very different. "Would you like some sex?" she asked.

I've been married to the same wonderful woman for almost four decades, and she's always been more than enough for me. I have never wanted to mess up the good thing I have, so I've regularly prayed, "God, in Jesus' name, help me to always be faithful to my dear wife. Always put it in my heart to say no to any temptation to stray. Help me always to glorify You in the way I conduct myself with and around other women."

On this night, I didn't pray. I basically just ran. Had you been there at that very moment, you might have heard some muffled laughter nearby.

I didn't know it, but a couple of my wonderful, godly staff had hidden behind a wall, waiting to see how I would respond to what they suspected was coming. They took great delight in seeing me squirm and run away.

I've thought about that scene in Budapest over the years. And though I felt no urge to fall into sin that night, it has occurred to me that a lot of men probably wouldn't have had the strength to keep walking. I don't say this to set myself up as some kind of wonderful man of God impervious to temptation, but to glorify the God who always keeps me safe and gives me strength when I'm in a place where temptation waits.

When we rationalize our sin, when we refuse to take responsibility for our choices and actions, in effect we're saying that God cannot help us to refuse the offers of evil that come our way. We're saying He can't really provide for us a way of escape from the temptations we face.

In other words, we're calling God a liar.

God never intended for us to battle temptation from a position of weakness. He never intended for us to throw up our hands and accept sin as part of our human existence. He didn't save us so we could just limp along in life, totally at the mercy of temptation and at the whim of a spiritual enemy who wants to build powerful strongholds in our lives.

He intended none of that for us. Do you know how He wants us to respond to the temptations that try to hook us? Read what the seventeenth-century Puritan writer John Owen wrote:

> As we have no strength to resist a temptation when it does come, when we are entered into it, but shall fall under it, without a supply of sufficiency of grace from God; so to reckon that we have no power or wisdom to keep ourselves from entering into temptation, but must be kept by the power and wisdom of God, is a preserving principle.[15]

If we intend to enjoy victory over temptation, we need to understand that *we can't do it on our own*. Apart from the power of Jesus Christ and the enabling of the Holy Spirit, we are no match for temptation or the devil. He's spent nearly all of human history working to tempt human beings into sinning against God. He knows far too much about us and about our natures for us to imagine that we can stand up to him on our own.

Although God does not and cannot entice us to sin, He most certainly allows powerful temptations to regularly cross our paths. Why? I believe He does so because it puts us in a place of greater dependence upon Him.

When the devil tried to tempt me to do evil that night in Budapest, the temptation never made it inside me—not because I'm above temptation (far from it), but because I resisted through Christ and stayed fast in my faith. I didn't rationalize my way into disobedience, but instead, relied on God's grace, which gave me the power to obey.

Jesus is mightier than sin. He is mightier than your sinful nature. He is mightier than any temptation the devil or this world can throw your way. And He is mightier than the strongholds the devil wants to set up in your life.

Love Conquers Temptation

I believe the greatest motivation to endure and overcome temptation is found in the epistle of James: "Blessed is the man who endures temptation; for when he has been approved, he will receive the crown of life which the Lord has promised to those who love Him" (1:12).

When you fail to love God with your whole heart, soul, mind, and strength, you leave yourself open to the attacks of the enemy. But when you love Him the way Jesus instructed us to, then you'll find the motivation to live as a man who consistently endures and overcomes temptation.

The devil wants you to rationalize your sin. It's one of the bricks he uses to construct his strongholds. But you don't have to stumble through life, languishing under the rule of one of his strongholds. When you fall in love with Jesus and stay in love with Him, the Lord will make you an overcomer. And no demonic stronghold can survive that kind of power.

6

The Devil Desires to Have You

A dark, malicious, unseen force does everything in its power to build as many strongholds in your life as possible. You are in a spiritual battle with a very real and crafty devil, and you can't win unless you recognize that fact and then take effective steps to counter it.

Satan desires to have you, just as he desired to have Simon Peter so long ago (Luke 22:31-32). His goal remains the same today as it was back then—to deceive you, trap you, ruin you, kill you.

And he's very good at what he does.

Satan's Résumé

Satan is your enemy, every bit as much as he was the enemy of Peter. So it's no surprise to hear Peter declare, "Be sober, be vigilant; because your adversary the devil walks about like a roaring lion, seeking whom he may devour" (1 Peter 5:8). The devil is your adversary, your personal antagonist. He is the fiercest and strongest opponent you will ever face. Erwin Lutzer, former pastor of The Moody Church in Chicago, wrote, "No matter how many pleasures

Satan offers you, his ultimate intention is to ruin you. Your destruction is his highest priority."[16]

Suppose you recommit your life to God after a season of drifting. You mean it with all your heart. Until then, you may have been coasting in exactly the wrong direction. You were like a dead fish being carried downstream.

Sometimes my children or grandchildren talk me into going to a water park to spend some time with them. They know I'm not going down any scary rides. I'm going to get an inner tube and head for the lazy river and go wherever it takes me. That's how the average Christian man is living, wherever this confused culture and the devil may take him.

But do you know what happens when you get out of the inner tube and start moving upstream against the tide? People will say, "Where are you going? I don't agree with that! Everybody else is going *this* way. You're narrow. You're a legalist!"

We're fighting an enemy who's out to destroy us, but people will call anyone who takes a stand against any sin a legalist. We live in crazy times.

Not only is Satan an adversary, but he is aggressive. He's on the hunt for unsuspecting and unprepared Christians. He's on the hunt for *you*. He's not passive. He's aggressively pursuing the damnation of your soul.

Satan annihilates. He doesn't play around. He plays for keeps. He's not out just to annoy you or irritate you or injure you, he's out to destroy you. He'll offer you something that you know is wrong, but sometimes you'll fall into his temptation anyway—and although he's the one who's been saying, "Do it, do it, do it," he'll turn around and violently accuse you as soon as you give in.

Then you may say, "God is making me feel really bad since I fell into this sin." But it's not God making you feel so bad. God is the one who wants you to come back into a close and warm relationship with Him. It's the devil who makes you feel so terrible. He hates you because God loves you. The devil doesn't want you happy, ever.

It's been said that Satan and the Savior cannot coexist in a believer's life, any more than light and darkness can. But even though Satan cannot possess a Christian, he can oppress him. The Bible teaches that he can defeat, discourage, and even devour the child of God. He will use any means available to ruin you (2 Corinthians 11:3).

The devil is a killer and the father of lies. Jesus said this about Satan: "He was a murderer from the beginning, and does not stand in the truth, because there is no truth in him. When he speaks a lie, he speaks from his own resources, for he is a liar and the father of it" (John 8:44). Not a single lie in this world originated from anyone but the devil himself. Whenever you lie, you climb in bed with Satan.

The devil lied to Eve in the Garden of Eden. The serpent said to the woman, "You will not surely die" for sinning against God, although God said she would (Genesis 3:4). Whenever someone stands up and says, "The Bible says," the devil immediately replies, "Oh, that's not what God said at all. How arrogant to think that your interpretation is the only one!"

Why do we buy such foolishness even for a second? Just try going on somebody's property posted with a no trespassing sign. Those who trespass *will* be prosecuted. The judge will say, "Sir, you went right by the sign."

"But I didn't know he actually meant *that*," you reply. "I have my own interpretation of the sign."

"That's nice," the judge will say. "Pay the fine and enjoy your own interpretation."

The Bible calls Satan "the prince of the power of the air" (Ephesians 2:2). Now, is a prince greater than a king? Hardly. Satan tries to present himself as a rival to God, the real King, but in fact, he's nowhere close.

The truth is, Satan never offers anything near to God's best, although he is an expert counterfeiter. The Bible says he "transforms himself into an angel of light" in order to peddle his false wares and deceive his victims (2 Corinthians 11:13-14). At best, though, he offers only a cheap counterfeit to God's perfect will.

Throughout history, Satan has offered many fine counterfeit religions. Many of them teach good morals and values, but all are devoid of the truth of the gospel. None of them can redeem you. Satan doesn't mind if you live a "good" life, just so long as he gets your soul in hell.

Earlier we talked about using bait that will lure a fish to bite the hook on the end of your fishing line. When you fish, you try to find a bait that can fool a fish—you use it to cover up the hook. That's exactly what the devil does. He doesn't show you the nasty hook. Instead, he shows you the attractive bait. You swallow it, and when you do, you end up getting snared by the hook.

I have a friend who graduated from college and seminary with me and went on to pastor a wonderful church. He got involved with a woman, lost his ministry, and is now cooking in a country restaurant. He didn't see the hook hidden by the bait.

These are the tactics of the enemy who wants to have you. He will try to deceive you into swallowing some attractive bait, and then he will use his hooks to pull you down, down, down into the abyss. You don't have to fall for his deceptions! Yes, the devil desires to have you, but you have an almighty Advocate who wants you even more. The apostle Peter made that wonderful discovery at perhaps the darkest moment of his life.

Coming Events

In the Old Testament, the devil and almighty God had a private conversation about Job's future troubles, but they didn't let him in on it. Later, however, Jesus let Simon in on a different conversation:

The Lord said, "Simon, Simon! Indeed, Satan has asked for you, that he may sift *you* as wheat. But I have prayed for you, that your faith should not fail; and when you have returned to Me, strengthen your brethren." But he said to Him, "Lord, I am ready to go with You, both to prison and to death." Then He said, "I tell you, Peter, the rooster shall not crow this day before you will deny three times that you know Me" (Luke 22:31-34).

Would it scare you if the Lord Jesus Christ spoke to you during your devotional time one morning and said, "The enemy is coming strong after you and I want you to know you're going to wilt"? Jesus revealed the enemy's plan to Peter, and the fisherman didn't believe Him.

Simon, Simon

Do you remember how John 1 describes the first time the Lord Jesus met Simon Peter? John the apostle was with Andrew, and when God saved the two of them, Andrew said, "I'm going to find my brother." When he found Peter, he told him, "I have found the Messiah, the Christ, the anointed one," and he brought his brother to Jesus. Jesus looked at Peter and said, "You are Simon."

The name *Simon* means "wavering one." Until then, Peter had been wavering, but at that moment, he came to Christ. Jesus then said to him, "From now on you will be called Cephas." *Cephas* means "a stone" (in Greek, *petros*, Peter). From that moment on, Simon became Peter.

So what was happening in Luke 22? If back in John 1 Jesus changed Simon's name to Peter, then why in this passage does Jesus call him Simon again? The answer is that even though Peter was a stone, in a very short while he would start wavering again.

Beware of any theology that has no room for a Christian wavering! We don't *want* to waver, but none of us are sinless. If you draw the line and say that every time a person backslides he's lost, your theology is in disagreement with Scripture. Don't you dare believe any theology that tells you a believer can lose his or her salvation.

But why did Jesus repeat Peter's name? Why did He say, "Simon, Simon"? When I was little and I went wrong, my mother would say, "Johnny Marshall, Johnny Marshall." I knew that when she repeated my name, she was not happy with me. Similarly, Jesus said, "Simon, Simon" because He knew Peter was about to deny Him three times.

The greatest and the most terrible definition I've ever heard of backsliding is this: You become artillery in the hands of Satan, aimed at the heart of God. George MacDonald said, "A man may sink by such slow degrees that, long after he is a devil, he may go on being a good churchman or a good dissenter, and thinking himself a good Christian."[17]

When we look around and compare ourselves with others, we usually think, *I'm not too bad.* That's the problem, however—to say that is to deceive ourselves. After Isaiah was touched by holy coals taken from God's heavenly altar, he said, "I am an unclean person. My lips are unclean." Then he said, "Good Lord, I am living among an unclean people" (see Isaiah 6:5).

Before you get touched by God, you think you're all right. You think your friends are all right. You think you're all right because you compare yourself with your friends. When God touches your life, however, you see that you're not right after all, and neither are your friends.

A Request to Sift

Jesus told Peter, "Satan has asked for you" (Luke 22:31). He asked for Peter specifically. The word "asked" means to beg something of someone.

Why was Satan *asking* God for Simon? He was asking because the enemy cannot touch one of God's children without God's permission.

We find that truth affirmed in the life of Job. Every time the Bible talks about what happened to Job, it names God as the one in charge. God gave Satan permission to touch Job's life, just as He did with Peter. If you belong to Jesus, the devil cannot touch you without first getting permission from God.

Jesus went on to say that the devil wanted to "sift [Peter] as wheat" (verse 31). To sift means "to winnow." In those days, workers would put their freshly harvested wheat in a big basket and shake it. As the contents of the basket were thrown upward into the wind, the chaff—the worthless hull around the wheat—would be blown away, leaving only the wheat to fall back into the basket.

The devil shakes the basket because he wants to show the world your worthlessness. He points to the chaff and says, "He may be wheat, but look at all the worthlessness in his life."

Jesus shakes the basket, too, but He does it so that the worthlessness leaves and you end up as pure wheat. "Johnny knows Me," Jesus says. "He's wheat, not chaff."

Faith produces wheat. Flesh produces chaff. One of the Puritans wrote, "Jesus uses a fan, and sifts to get rid of the chaff, but the devil uses a fan and sifts to get rid of the wheat."[18]

Even as Christians we tend to be very judgmental. When an apparently godly person does something evil, we often say, "What he did was wrong. *I* would never do that. He's a godless person."

Not necessarily! The Bible calls David a man after God's own heart, even though David had committed adultery and murder. There was a time David followed God wholeheartedly. But he got careless, and in the sifting process, the worthlessness came out. Would you believe there was still potential in David for real, glorious wheat? Absolutely. But his carelessness cost him big time.

When a well-known Christian falls morally, news reports don't start out by saying, "This person's global ministry has touched thousands of lives and blessed people around the world." No, they don't.

They always go straight to the chaff. But what about all the good the fallen person ever did? The devil doesn't want anyone to see or remember that.

"I Have Prayed for You"

Jesus interceded for Peter. He told him, "I have prayed for you" (Luke 22:32).

The word "prayed" comes from a root term that means "binding." Jesus was saying, "I'm getting involved in this. I have committed Myself to you as your bondsman, your surety. The devil has asked for you, but I'm asking My Father for you. I'm putting a bind on this. I'm committing Myself to you as your bondsman."

You may be going through tough times right now, but I want to remind you that the Lord Jesus Christ ever lives to intercede for you. If you're in a difficult situation, He's praying for you. He's binding Himself to you. He's your surety. And if you'll trust Him, He'll bring you through.

Simon needed that good word. You also need to know there's light at the end of the tunnel and that it's not a Mack truck barreling down on you.

Jesus intervened for Simon. He said, "I have prayed for you, *that your faith will not fail*" (verse 32). Some people say that Peter's faith failed. No, it didn't. His flesh failed. Your flesh will fail you too. Faith doesn't fail. If your faith failed, you'd be out of God's family. Peter's hope may have died to some extent. His courage may have failed. His flesh certainly failed, as it will fail us. But genuine faith never fails. And Jesus is praying that your faith is genuine.

The Lord Knows

Do you recall the scene at the end of John's Gospel when Jesus showed up on the beach after Simon Peter and the rest of the disciples had gone back to fishing? Jesus said to them, "Come over here. I'm going to fix you breakfast." They came, and Jesus questioned Peter.

How many times did Peter deny Christ? Three. How many times did Jesus ask Peter whether he loved Him? Three. Do you think Peter made any connection there?

Not long before, Peter felt supremely confident in himself. "Everybody else may go away," he boasted, "but I'll never leave You. I'll follow You to prison and worse." Later, on the beach, after the third time Jesus asked Peter, "Do you love Me?" Peter finally gave the right answer: "Lord, You know."

Why would he give that answer? Because the last time the two spoke, Jesus told Peter he was going to blow it, and Peter insisted he wouldn't. But Jesus said, "Yes you will." Jesus knew, and Peter didn't. So now Peter's thinking, *You're asking me if I love You? I thought I knew before, and I didn't. But You know.*

Jeremiah had it right when he declared that our hearts are "desperately" wicked (17:9). Who can know our hearts? Only God. That's why I love the verse that says, "The Lord knows those who are His" (2 Timothy 2:19). How glad I am that He does!

Peter's Big Mistake

Peter was mistaken to have confidence in himself. He appears to have thought, *Self is sufficient. If You pray for me, Jesus, I can get through this on my own.*

You may say, "I'd never do that." Don't be so sure! Satan always attacks at the point where a man is too sure of himself.

A study by Temple University revealed that a burglar's most likely entry point is the front door. If I were going to burglarize a home, I would think it'd be better to go around to the back door or through a side window, and not until dark. It's true that burglars will utilize back doors and windows if necessary, but they use the front door significantly more than any other entry point. Why? Because many people leave it unlocked.

Most of us expect Satan to try to sneak into our lives through a little-known back door, but in reality, his tactics mirror those of professional thieves. That's how most men fall morally. Self-sufficiency will blind you from your own infirmities and weaknesses. Most of us are weaker than we think, particularly in three areas: wine, women, and wealth.

What's the usual counsel today about alcohol? "Drink in moderation." Tell that to the 16 million confirmed alcoholics in the United States![19] Have you ever thought about the vindictiveness of alcohol? Do you think anyone gets up in the morning and says, "I'm so happy today, I'm going to ruin my life with this bottle of whiskey. I have it under control"?

I drank for nine years, so I've been there. The "moderation" line has to come from someone who doesn't know what alcohol will do to you. Read Proverbs 23:29-35. It tells you that if you drink enough booze, it will make you feel like a man on top of a sailboat's mast. It also warns that alcohol will whop you like a man whopping you. Even so, when you get up from being whopped, you'll want another drink. Now, why on earth would anybody want to drink something that just whopped him?

Proverbs 20:1 calls wine "a mocker" and strong drink "a brawler" and says that those who drink them are "led astray." How in God's name can I justify drinking something that mocks me? And by the way, why do I need something to give me a buzz when I have the Holy Spirit?

Have you ever done anything shameful and said afterward, "I can't believe I did that"? You shocked yourself. You didn't know that something so ugly was in you. Simon Peter said, "I thought I was following the Lord as close as I could. I wouldn't have believed anyone who told me I was going to curse and swear and cut off someone's ear." And yet that's exactly what he did.

Call It Restoration

Although Peter had fallen back into living like Simon, at least he had the courage to follow Jesus into the courtyard the night before the crucifixion. Yes, that's where he fell to temptation; but only a brave man would have gone even that far. He failed terribly. But a short while later, on Pentecost, Peter preached about the risen Christ and 3000 souls were saved.

God really changed him, didn't He?

But wait a minute—do you mean someone can be Simon, get changed to Peter, start acting like Simon again, and then have the ministry of Peter once more? Yes! If that's not restoration, I don't know my Bible.

After Pentecost, when the Jewish leaders that made up the Sanhedrin tried to silence the apostles from sharing the gospel, Peter stood boldly before them and proclaimed, "Whether it is right in the sight of God to listen to you more than to God, you judge. For we cannot but speak the things which we have seen and heard" (Acts 4:19-20). Scottish minister Robert Murray McCheyne said, "It's not great talent God blesses so much as great likeness to Jesus."[20]

You may not be a singer, preacher, Sunday school teacher, or leader, but you're a man in whom God lives, or in whom God desires to live. If you've come to Him, He will use you. But you need to come to Him.

Come On Home

Are you far from Jesus? If so, do you want to come home?

You need the Father's embrace. You need the joy of your sonship restored. Maybe you used to talk to people about God, but now you feel so overwhelmingly defeated that you just can't imagine it. You have a good memory, though. You remember what it used to be like before you wound up in the hog pen.

Ask God to forgive you. Tell him you're tired of being where you are. Admit you're sick of living as you have been. Tell Him, "I'm ready for a change."

Jesus Christ has omniscient, penetrating eyes. When He does a work in your life, He sees you not only for who you are, but also for who you could become. I've been a Christian and a preacher for long enough to know this as a fact.

What if right now the Lord Jesus Christ would speak out loud, wherever you are, call out your name, and put your face on a big screen? The lights would go down. Everybody would get quiet and nobody would be judgmental because we'd all realize we might be the next one on the screen.

The Lord Jesus would tell you how He sees you today. You'd probably sit there stunned, like I would. I'll bet we'd weep. But then He would say, "My child, don't be discouraged. I can not only change your name, I can change your life. Let Me show you who you can become."

I believe if God would show you what your life could be like, you would get on your face before Him and praise the Lord for who He is.

Let's go back in time. I'm eighteen years old. I quit school at age sixteen. I almost died in a car accident, along with another person. I was driving while heavily under the influence. Not only could I have been killed that night, but in the back seat of the car I had a shotgun.

Earlier that day, I'd raced a guy in my GTO. That night, I got into a little scuffle at a drive-in with the guy I had raced and two others. I said, "We know how to deal with more than one." This is how stupid I was back then. I left to go home and get my gun, put it in the back seat of my car, and said, "We're headed back to the drive-in."

In my highly intoxicated state, I drifted off to the side of the road, and when I jerked my steering wheel to get back onto the road, instantly I knew we were in trouble. The last thing I remember is taking God's name in vain. The car flipped several times and slid toward oncoming traffic.

All I can say is that God spared my life. Had I died that night, I'd be in hell right now. But God had mercy on me. So do you know what I did?

The next day, I got on crutches. When they took me out to see the car, I walked by it and said, "I tell you, you just can't kill me, can you?" I was one arrogant punk.

I returned to the pool room a few days later. Guys put up money on me because I was a good pool player. I played in tournaments, hundred-dollar nine ball. It doesn't sound like much today, but more than four decades ago, a hundred dollars was a lot of money. We'd play and drink, get drunk, curse, swear, steal, and spend the night in jail for drunk driving. I lost my license for a year. Dad had checked out when I was seven years old and Mom was working two jobs and raising six kids by herself. She was gone in the morning and gone at night. I'd come home alone, get drunk, and puke.

And God looked down and said, "Johnny Simon…"

He saw me for who I was—hell bound, lost, cursing Him, swearing, stealing, living in a project. And God, because He has omniscient, penetrating eyes, looked down and thought, *Anointed preacher, pastoring a church in Northwest Atlanta.*

At that point, however, I knew only who I was. Satan continued to say, "This is all you'll ever be, boy. Everybody you know is living like this."

I didn't know then that I'd repent and ask God to forgive me. God had a whole new world out there for me, a brand new life, the life I was chosen for. I just lacked the sense to know how much God loved me.

Don't let the devil keep you from coming home. Don't allow any of his strongholds to trap you any longer. Come home! And experience the life God has chosen for you.

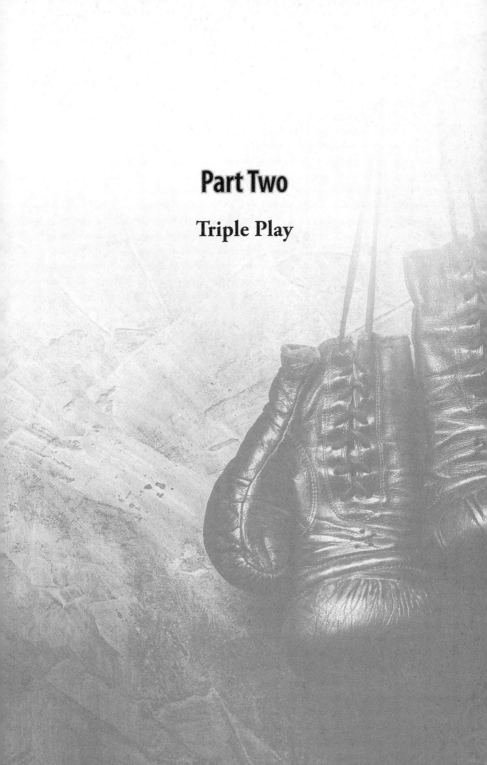

Part Two

Triple Play

7

Sex: The Drama of Seduction

Some time ago I had one of those conversations I wished I could have avoided. The subject? A thirty-six-year-old pastor I had mentored who had been leading a dynamic, growing church… right up until he decided to leave his wife and children to marry his eighteen-year-old secretary.

Heartbroken over what this young man had done, I asked the former preacher's wife about how this could have happened. "Did you not see something going on in your husband's life?" I asked.

With tears in her eyes, she answered, "I could tell there was something going on. I saw an attraction between them, but I didn't know what to do. I tried to tell him what I was seeing, and he would get so mad at me that he started cursing at me. I told him, 'You just need to be aware.'"

I wish I could say this kind of story rarely happens. I wish I could say that all professing Christian men remain faithful to their wives and avoid sexual sin. But I know that's not reality—and I grieve over it.

A Field Day for the Devil

One of the most difficult parts of my job as the pastor of a large church is to hear the many stories of destruction, heartache, broken homes, shattered marriages, ruined reputations, and lost ministries that are all caused by sexual sin. Study after sad study shows that the rates of marital infidelity (a nice term for what God calls adultery) and divorce in the church today closely resemble those that exist in the secular world.

It has become painfully obvious that Satan is having his way in the hearts and minds of far too many Christian men. What they don't understand is that he is using this sexual carnage to build strongholds in their lives that he will use to ruin them.

One of my favorite Bible verses says, "No temptation has overtaken you except such as is common to man; but God is faithful, who will not allow you to be tempted beyond what you are able, but with the temptation will also make the way of escape, that you may be able to bear it" (1 Corinthians 10:13). God promises here that though sin tempts all of us, He is faithful to give us a way to get past every temptation.

Let's look for a moment at this verse from a masculine viewpoint. Sexual temptation is nearly universal. Take a quick look around you and see how the world lives. The latest statistics indicate that more than a third of married men cheat on their wives and that more than half of all marriages will be impacted by marital infidelity. And adultery isn't the only sexual sin rampant in our world. Far from it!

Pornography has become a multibillion dollar industry in the United States. Some estimate that around forty million adults in the United States regularly visit porn sites. One national news website reported that "porn sites get more visitors each month than Netflix, Amazon, and Twitter combined."[21]

Unfortunately, Christians aren't immune to the seduction of the soul-destroying filth called pornography. One poll showed that nearly half of Christians surveyed called pornography a major problem in their home, while 55 percent of American Christian men admitted to looking at pornography in the previous month. Another survey showed that 77 percent—more than three-quarters—of Christian men between the ages of eighteen and thirty view pornography (easily accessible on countless websites) at least once a month, with 36 percent looking at it every day.[22] Depending on which study you believe, between 10 and 50 percent of Christian men admit they are addicted to pornography.

The devil is having a field day perverting God's purpose for sex, and he's using that perversion to place strongholds in the lives of thousands of Christian men. Never forget that Satan's goal is "to steal, and to kill, and to destroy" (John 10:10). He's accomplishing that goal in large part by tempting men into all sorts of sexual immorality.

I long for Christian men to see that God has something *much* better for us. He wants to empower us to tear down strongholds of sexual sin so that we can enjoy His gift of sex to the fullest. His Word contains the wisdom that can empower us to stay pure in our sexual lives, or to become pure once more if we've already given in to hell's seductions.

I Wish I Knew Then...

I can't even count the number of men who have approached me at church or at a men's conference and said something like, "I wish I knew back when I decided to get involved in sexual sin what I know now. I've been through hell on earth, and not a day goes by that I don't wish I could go back and undo what I've done."

After listening to man after man telling me about the terrible consequences of his sexual sin, I've realized that most men have no idea what's in store for them when they get into an adulterous relationship or begin a sexual relationship outside of marriage. They get into the sin, looking for everything from illicit pleasure to acceptance from a woman, not understanding the price they will pay.

But the Bible teaches that there is an "afterward." It also emphasizes the importance of looking ahead to see where your actions will lead you. Solomon offered his son this wisdom: "Ponder the path of your feet" (Proverbs 4:26). In other words, think about the consequences of your actions.

Nobody with a functioning brain would spend the money to buy an airplane ticket without knowing its destination. Why, then, should it be any different with our decisions regarding sex? And yet untold numbers of men board a flight thinking it leads to seductive Hawaii, when in fact it lands (if it doesn't crash) in soul-crushing Haiti. That's why the Bible so repeatedly warns men against sexual sin, especially adultery.

The price for sexual sin of any kind can be very high, yet if we're not on our guard, any of us is capable of it. All it takes is one stupid moment, and your life, and the lives of so many around you, can be altered forever and in terrible ways.

Far too many of us just don't heed God's warnings against sexual sin. We don't listen to what God has to say about sex in His Word, refuse to heed sound biblical teaching, and ignore the mistakes of those before us who have crashed on the road to sexual immorality.

Solomon confessed to his son, "How I have hated instruction, and my heart despised correction! I have not obeyed the voice of my teachers, nor inclined my ear to those who instructed me!" (Proverbs 5:12-13). This sounds like the lament of a man who recognizes and regrets his sexual sins, whose head swims with thoughts of, *If only I had listened...*

God has given you everything you need to keep yourself from allowing sexual sin to build a stronghold in your life. He's given you His Word, which contains wisdom from those who kept themselves strong and pure as well as warnings from those who wrote of their mistakes and sins (so that you won't make the same ones).

Guard Your Eyes and Your Mind

Science has proven that men are generally more "visual" than women, especially in regard to sexual attraction. When you pass a beautiful woman on the street, don't you often turn for that second look? Be honest! Sure, a woman will turn and give a look to a handsome man, but for guys, it's nearly *always* about what we see.

As a pastor who has done his share of premarital counseling, I've seen more examples of this than I care to count. The young couple comes to my office, and after some icebreaking conversation, I ask how they met and what attracted them to each other.

The young woman almost always will say, "Well, it's funny you should ask, Pastor. We were in the same Sunday school department for years, and I never really noticed him. But as we spent time together in group gatherings, I could just tell that he was a kind-hearted, thoughtful guy. I just couldn't help falling for him."

Then comes Bubba's answer: "Goodness, Pastor, just *look* at her! She's stunning! The first time I saw her, I thought she was the most beautiful girl in all creation, and I said to myself, 'I'm going to marry that girl one day.'"

I'm not sure why God saw fit to wire men this way, but I know that the temptation to sin sexually most often gets a foothold inside us first through what we see, and only later through what we think. In other words, we see it, our mind starts dwelling on it, and then we feel a strong temptation to go and get it.

Remember the story of how King David fell into sin? The king committed adultery with Bathsheba, the wife of his faithful servant, Uriah. After David discovered that Bathsheba had become pregnant because of their affair, he tried everything to cover up his wrongdoing, including sending Uriah into a dangerous war zone, where he died.

David didn't just wake up one morning and decide to ruin his life, as well as the lives of others caught up in the consequences of his sin. He didn't walk onto his palace rooftop bent on adultery.

The Bible tells us, "Then it happened one evening that David arose from his bed and walked on the roof of the king's house. And from the roof *he saw a woman bathing,* and the woman *was very beautiful to behold.* So David sent and inquired about the woman" (2 Samuel 11:2-3).

David's temptation to commit sexual sin didn't start much differently than it does for millions of men around the world every day. He saw a beautiful woman, probably watched her for some time, and then his mind fed his unrighteous desires. Before long, his body followed. The result was an enormous, embarrassing, shameful mess with repercussions and consequences not just for David himself, but for his whole family and his entire kingdom.

Jesus addressed the connection between what we allow our eyes to see and sexual purity when He told His followers, "I say to you that whoever looks at a woman to lust for her has already committed adultery with her in his heart. If your right eye causes you to sin, pluck it out and cast it from you; for it is more profitable for you that one of your members perish, than for your whole body to be cast into hell" (Matthew 5:28-29).

That's a huge issue for many of us, isn't it? And not just because we're visual creatures, but because in today's world, it's nearly impossible to keep our eyes off of things that cause our minds to wander where they shouldn't. Just about every form of media today—television, music, movies, magazines, even billboards—presents us with seductive images that can trigger thoughts of sexual sin.

This is one area where we as Christian men need to be doing some *serious* spiritual battle. It has been said that the mind is our strongest sexual organ. A battle rages daily for control of that organ. That means we need to bring "every thought into captivity to the obedience of Christ" (2 Corinthians 10:5). It also suggests that we need to follow the example of Job, a man the Bible calls "blameless and upright, and one who feared God and shunned evil" (Job 1:1). That godly man said, "I made a covenant with my eyes not to look lustfully at a young woman" (Job 31:1 NIV).

Have you ever made such a covenant with your eyes? If not, why not?

Think of the Consequences!

All sins against God carry consequences. Sexual sin is no different; in fact, it's probably no stretch to say that the earthly consequences of sexual sin last longer and reach further than any other sin.

That explains why the apostle Paul wrote, "Flee sexual immorality. Every sin that a man does is outside the body, but he who commits sexual immorality sins against his own body" (1 Corinthians 6:18).

It's true that all sins offend God, corrupt us, and put distance between us and our Creator. Sexual sin is just one of many offenses that can bar us from God's eternal kingdom. But sexual sin differs from the others in that it takes an act that God created as a means for married couples to share their hearts, their souls, and their bodies, and instead uses it to damage people physically, mentally, and spiritually. Sexual sin can and will ruin your life, not just because of the temporal consequences (STDs, broken relationships, unplanned pregnancies, etc.), but because it places a potent and relentless stronghold within you.

I once sat at my desk and wrote down a long list of the consequences of sexual sin. I call it my "detriment list." The list includes things like bringing reproach to my Lord Jesus Christ, but it also includes hurting the people I love (my amazing wife and my beautiful daughters, for starters), what it would cost me and my ministry, how it would bring me and the church I serve to public disgrace, and a host of other things that I consider vitally important.

As I've read over that list, I've come to a simple conclusion: It's not worth it.

Solomon once rehearsed to his son the many dangers and consequences of sexual immorality. He knew about these things personally, both because of the sins of his father and because of his own wrongdoings. He knew firsthand about the devastation sexual sin brings, so he wrote this bit of wisdom about a loose woman: "Remove your way far from her, and do not go near the door of her house, lest you give your honor to others, and your years to the cruel one" (Proverbs 5:8-9).

What does it mean to give one's years to the cruel one? It refers to losing everything you've accumulated and marring every good accomplishment you had during the best and most productive years of your life. I take Solomon's warning very seriously, and I'd encourage any man faced with sexual temptation to do the same.

I've been married to Janet for nearly fifty years, and I love her more every day we're together. I've also been a Baptist minister for forty years, and I still love what I do. Not only that, but Janet loves being the wife of a Baptist minister—of *this* Baptist minister, I should say—and my children and my grandchildren all love that I'm a preacher.

God made sure I'd have a good thing going in this life, and I'm more grateful for that than I can put into words. It's a great honor and privilege to serve the Son of God. It is also a great pleasure to have such a wonderful, beautiful woman as my partner in ministry, my best friend, and my lover.

I know the terrible consequences for sexual sin. I've seen it too often. That is why I ask God every day to remind me of this truth, and to strengthen me against any sexual stronghold the enemy may try to build in my heart.

We Need to Talk

Some time back, my wife came to me and said, "I need to talk to you about something."

I think I can speak for most men when I say that hearing your wife say those words strikes fear into your heart. Immediately I started thinking, *What have I done now?* I felt so shaken up that I started praying and repenting of sins I hadn't even committed. I even started repenting of *other* people's sins!

I think my wife could see a state of near-panic in my eyes and she immediately let me know that I hadn't done anything wrong.

"Honey, there's no accusation here," she said. Immediately I exhaled. "It's just a warning," she continued. I stopped breathing again.

"There's a lady in the church who I think has got her eyes set on you," she explained. "I wasn't going to bring this up, but two other ladies noticed it too. I just want you to know this, so you can see for yourself that everywhere you are at church, she is too."

I frankly doubted the truth of what Janet told me. At the time, I wouldn't have said she was wrong, but I still needed to see it for myself.

Sure enough, at church the following Sunday, I saw it. Everywhere I went that morning—to the fellowship hall, to the sanctuary immediately after the service, to the pastor's reception line—there she was. When I glanced over at her, she'd smile back in a way that made me uncomfortable.

I recognized Satan was trying to set a trap for me, and though this woman presented no real temptation for me, I knew that the situation had the potential to become something that felt uncomfortable and looked bad. The Bible tells us to "abstain from all appearance of evil" (1 Thessalonians 5:22 KJV), so on the very day I recognized the problem, my wife and I prayed and committed the situation to God. I thank God the Holy Spirit broke the power of whatever the devil might have been trying to do.

Solomon wrote, "Though one may be overpowered by another, two can withstand him. And a threefold cord is not quickly broken" (Ecclesiastes 4:12). The message behind this verse is simple: There's strength in numbers.

I've learned that it's important for me, or for any married man who wants to win over sexual temptation, to make himself accountable to his wife. When I make myself accountable to Janet and to Jesus (a powerful threefold cord!), then it's a good bet that temptation won't overpower me. That is why I've always made accountability part of my battle plan against sin and temptation. It's also why I encourage my brothers in Christ to do the same thing (for more on this, see chapter 14).

A Good Time for a Hasty Retreat

During my studies at Southeastern Baptist Theological Seminary, one of my professors said something that I'll never forget. It has proven extremely valuable to me over the years. Standing in front of a classroom full of young, aspiring preachers, he said, "Anybody can have an affair."

Many Christian men tend to think of themselves as too smart, too strong, too spiritual to ever fall into sexual sin, but I can tell you they're wrong. The devil knows our weaknesses, and he knows we are susceptible to all sorts of sexual sin. He knows that if he can't get us to commit adultery or fornication, he still has all sorts of other options. That's why God gave us this important bit of wisdom to help us to stay sexually pure: "Remove your way far from her, and do not go near the door of her house" (Proverbs 5:7). In the New Testament, the apostle Paul put it this way: "Flee sexual immorality" (1 Corinthians 6:18). Don't stand and argue with it, don't bargain with it, don't attempt to rebuke it in the name of Jesus. Just get away as fast as you can.

I can't think of a better biblical example of fleeing sexual immorality than the Old Testament hero Joseph (Genesis 39:1-12). As a slave in Egypt, Joseph earned the respect and honor of his masters, who had received amazing blessings from God due to their association with Joseph.

One day, as handsome young Joseph tended to his duties in the home of his master, Potiphar, the master's wife, brazenly propositioned Joseph—not once but twice. The second time, she became very aggressive (sexual temptation doesn't change much, does it?).

The woman's aggressiveness was no match for Joseph's commitment to his God, however. Joseph "left his garment in her hand, and fled and ran outside" (Genesis 39:12).

How many men do you know who would have had the strength and character to do what Joseph did? I doubt very many, unfortunately. What gave Joseph the strength to act as he did? You see the answer in his response to the woman's advances: "How then can I do this great wickedness, and sin against God?" (Genesis 39:9). Joseph loved God more than he loved any pleasure he thought he might get from an illicit hookup. He saw an affair as less, not more. And that outlook is what helped to make him a hero.

The Look of Love

The day Janet and I got married, she was all of seventeen years and seventeen days old. Folks often got married back then at much younger ages than they do now. I say with joy and gratitude that I've enjoyed every day I've had with her. I still rejoice over the gift God gave me in Janet, and I can honestly say that she's still all I want and more.

That's just the way God intended it to be.

When most people think of word pictures of married sexual intimacy in the Bible, their minds automatically go to the Song of Solomon. But the following passage uses poetic and even erotic imagery to both warn and encourage men of God to find sexual satisfaction *only* with their wives:

> Drink water from your own cistern,
>   running water from your own well.
> Should your springs overflow in the streets,

> your streams of water in the public squares?
> Let them be yours alone,
>> never to be shared with strangers (Proverbs 5:15-17
>> NIV).

Have you ever been so thirsty that the only thing that would satisfy was a tall glass of cold water? Solomon's words tell us that we can have that water, but that it must come from a single source only, a source that is yours and yours alone, never to be shared. Solomon then tells his son:

> May your fountain be blessed,
>> and may you rejoice in the wife of your youth.
> A loving doe, a graceful deer—
>> may her breasts satisfy you always,
>> may you ever be intoxicated with her love (Proverbs
>> 5:18-19).

Immediately following this passage comes a warning about and an encouragement to fidelity: "Why, my son, be intoxicated with another man's wife? Why embrace the bosom of a wayward woman?" (Proverbs 5:20).

Solomon asks a rhetorical question here; the answer is obvious. He wants to point out to every young male reader that God has provided him with everything he needs for sexual satisfaction—in the form of his wife. Cheating will get him nothing but sorrow.

For Blessing and Protection

Sometimes I just want to grab some men by their lapels and shout at them: "When are you going to get it through your thick skull that God didn't put limitations on sex because He doesn't want you to have any fun? He did it because He wants to bless you and protect you!"

God isn't in the least against sexual pleasure. He created sex not just for reproduction, but also for enjoyment. The Lord didn't put the wall of marriage around sex to rob us of good times, but to increase the pleasure of sex within the confines of marriage.

When married or unmarried men seek sexual satisfaction anywhere but within marriage, they set themselves up not only for disappointment and disillusionment, but they also make themselves vulnerable to sexual strongholds—some of the toughest to bring down. But when they honor sex by treating it the way God instructs them to in His Word, God frees them to experience ever-increasing enjoyment and enrichment in their sex lives.

Do you know the best way to bring down a tough sexual stronghold? Never let it get built in the first place.

8

Money: The Lure of Greed

Bernie Madoff was a gifted, intelligent, influential member of the US financial industry. He founded and served as chairman of Bernard L. Madoff Investment Securities, LLC, which had a long and impressive list of clients. He helped launch the NASDAQ stock market and also served on the board of the National Association of Securities Dealers and as an advisor to the Securities and Exchange Commission.

For a long time, the name Madoff carried a lot of clout on Wall Street. Experts in his industry respected and admired him as an innovator who consistently served his clients well.

Who knew that underneath all the impressive exterior, Madoff was in fact a thief, a swindler, and a liar who would end up conning thousands of investors out of $65 billion? He used a Ponzi scheme, which uses the money of later investors to pay off earlier investors—recruiting new investor Peter to pay off old investor Paul. What he did was unethical, immoral, and highly illegal.

I have a friend who tells me his mother frequently quoted to him a particular Bible verse whenever she suspected him of wrongdoing:

"You may be sure that your sin will find you out" (Numbers 32:23). Madoff's crimes got exposed when some of his clients demanded a total of $7 billion in returns. Madoff didn't have it, not by a long shot. When he informed his sons, who worked for his firm, that he intended to pay the returns, they demanded to know where he would get the money. He then confessed that one branch of the firm was nothing more than a complicated Ponzi scheme.

Madoff's sons immediately reported their father to federal authorities, and on December 11, 2008, he was arrested and charged with securities fraud. The following March, Madoff pled guilty to 11 felonies. A judge later sentenced him to 150 years in prison.

How could a man like Madoff, who seemed to have it all, fall the way he did? How could such a gifted, talented, and *very* wealthy man go from being one of the most admired and respected businessmen in America to becoming the most reviled criminal in the US financial industry?

I believe the answer to that question can be summed up in one simple word: greed.

In the 1987 movie *Wall Street*, the key character, a Wall Street financier named Gordon Gekko, infamously says, "Greed, for lack of a better word, is good." He then lists all the benefits he believes the world has enjoyed through greed.

Contrary to Gordon Gekko and Bernie Madoff, greed is *not* good. Greed lives at the heart of countless scandals and crimes in world history. Even in the Bible, we see how greed led to countless sins responsible for untold pain and suffering. The Word of God issues many strong warnings about the destructive power of greed and materialism. In fact, greed is such a serious offense that the Bible highlights it as one of the sins that will bar people from God's eternal kingdom (see 1 Corinthians 6:9-11).

Thank God I'm not Bernie Madoff, you might think. Yes, thank God. But Bernie Madoff the admired businessman didn't set out to become Bernie Madoff the reviled criminal. Greed has a way of changing a man into something he never wanted to be.

Any man.

The Love of Money: A Warning

I don't know Bernie Madoff, so I can't tell you when he started going wrong. Did he always have a problem with greed? Did he always struggle with unscrupulous behavior? Or did a lust for things and piles and piles of money at some point turn his heart into mush? As a younger man, did he ever imagine that one day he'd morph into a villain hated by millions?

I think, however, I can safely say this: Madoff, for all his gifted-ness and success, got overtaken by what the Bible calls "the love of money." His unbridled greed motivated him to do things decent people would never even consider. He is a tragic, spot-on example of the kind of man the apostle Paul described in his letter to a young pastor named Timothy:

> Those who desire to be rich fall into temptation and a snare, and into many foolish and harmful lusts which drown men in destruction and perdition. For the love of money is a root of all kinds of evil, for which some have strayed from the faith in their greediness, and pierced themselves through with many sorrows (1 Timothy 6:9-10).

The last verse in this passage gets misquoted more than just about any in the Bible. No doubt you've heard people say, "Money is the root of all evil." But that's not what Paul wrote. Money, in and of itself, is neither good nor evil. It is, in fact, a tool—one we can use for good (caring for ourselves and our families or supporting worthy ministries or missionary organizations, both of which the Bible commends) or for evil (buying pornography, alcohol, drugs, gambling).

Paul didn't condemn money itself, nor did he condemn working hard to make more of it. In fact, the Bible actually *encourages* hard work, earning, and enjoying the fruits of one's labor. It tells us that God blesses the disciplined, those who feel motivated enough to work hard. Solomon wrote, "It is good and fitting for one to eat and drink, and to enjoy the good of all of his labor in which he toils under the sun all of the days of his life which God gives him, for it is his heritage" (Ecclesiastes 5:18).

The Bible, however, warns against greed, against what Paul called "the love of money." The apostle warned Timothy and his church that when a man turns his life focus to becoming rich, he has run his ship aground. He has become guilty of loving money, which will send him headlong into temptation and all sorts of sin. A focus on material wealth can easily become a stronghold so devastating that it can pave the way to a man's eternal damnation.

The book you're holding in your hands focuses on destroying spiritual strongholds. Paul's words to Timothy fit like a hand in a glove with what I'm trying to say here. He uses words—"temptation," "snare," and "many foolish and harmful lusts"—that all point to the strongholds the Bible tells us to avoid, escape, and destroy.

Like sex, money is a good gift from God. When we handle these gifts in the way He has ordained, we put ourselves in a perfect position to receive God's very best in those areas. But when we allow the devil, working with our own selfish desires, to build strongholds of lust or materialism or the love of money, we open ourselves up to fall into countless other sins. Maybe we begin engaging in unethical or illegal business practices. Maybe we allow our hearts to be consumed with jealousy or envy. Perhaps we become increasingly selfish, or start to neglect our families and ministries. The love of money has a way of capturing our hearts, which is why it so often leads to idolatry (Colossians 3:5). In other words, it shoves aside God Himself. We make our hearts into temples of greed where we worship the great god money.

If that's not a stronghold, I don't know what is.

While the love of money won't necessarily put us in prison, as it did Bernie Madoff, it does rob us of everything good that our loving God wants to give us.

Biblical Wisdom about Money

If you were to go door to door through your neighborhood to invite unchurched people to visit your church, and you were to ask them why they don't attend, I can guarantee you that among other objections, you'll hear this one: "I'd like to go to church, but I want to go to one that doesn't talk so much about money."

As a longtime pastor, I try to be as sensitive as possible to the needs of the individuals in my congregation, as well as to the needs of those in my sphere of influence who need to hear the gospel. At the same time, I know I have to preach the whole Word of God and not just what people want to hear. I have to ask, "What does God tell me they *need* to hear?"

I've spent more hours than I can count studying the Bible. And while I don't claim to know or fully understand everything the Lord put in His Word, I can tell you this: A great many of the words recorded in the Bible address money and material wealth. Some have estimated that more than 2000 Bible verses address money.

Jesus Himself spoke more about money than He did about heaven and hell combined. Most of Jesus' parables deal in some way with money or material possessions. Not only that, but many of His other teachings also address money. Some of them directly confront materialism and the love of money.

Jesus once warned His followers against the trap of loving money. "No one can serve two masters," He said, "for either he will hate the one and love the other, or else he will be loyal to the one and despise the other. You cannot serve God and mammon" (Matthew 6:24). The term "mammon" can be translated as "worldly riches." Jesus is letting us know that we cannot be loyal both to Him and to the pursuit of money. If we love money, then we will despise God. And what does it look like when you love money?

More Is Never Enough

I recently read a poll that summarized how people think about money. The poll broke down people's income levels and asked them how much more they thought they needed to make a comfortable living. Many, if not most, of the respondents said they needed to make more.

How much more did those who make $50,000 a year need to have? The average answer came to about $25,000 more, meaning the respondents believed they needed $75,000 to live comfortably. When those who made $100,000 a year were asked the same question, the answers ranged up to $250,000 annually.

Have you ever asked yourself how much money you'd need to make in order to be happy? Would it be enough to afford a bigger house in a nicer neighborhood? Enough to buy a brand new car every year or two? Enough to send your kids to the finest (most expensive) university in the country?

Though Satan and the world would love you to believe that your happiness depends on making more money, the Bible teaches that those who love money will never make enough to feel satisfied and happy. Solomon, who accumulated a staggering amount of wealth and power as Israel's second king, learned this lesson the hard way. He wrote, "He who loves silver will not be satisfied with silver; nor he who loves abundance, with increase. This also is vanity" (Ecclesiastes 5:10).

Did you notice the word Solomon chose to describe the pursuit of worldly riches? *Vanity*. Trying to find happiness or fulfillment in worldly riches, he says, is an act of futility. It's like trying to catch the wind in your hand.

John D. Rockefeller, the founder of Standard Oil and the man considered the richest person in modern history (at the time of his death in 1937, his net worth was $1.4 billion, equivalent to $23 billion in today's dollars), had some very telling things to say about the accumulation of worldly riches. "I have made many millions," he said, "but they brought me no happiness."[23] Later he declared, "The poorest man I know is the man who has nothing but money."[24]

A proverb often quoted in the ancient Roman world goes like this: "Money is like seawater. The more you drink, the thirstier you get." No doubt the idea originated from someone who had wasted a good chunk of his life making himself a slave to money. You can't find fulfillment and happiness that way. Pursuing riches puts you on a road leading only to futility and emptiness.

Solomon also had learned that protecting and maintaining worldly wealth creates a lot of stress: "The sleep of a laboring man is sweet, whether he eats little or much; but the abundance of the rich will not permit him to sleep" (Ecclesiastes 5:12). Solomon says that monetary wealth can cause you a lot of sleepless nights.

William Henry Vanderbilt probably would agree with Solomon. The famous businessman, who inherited $100 million from his father and later increased his fortune to almost $194 million, once lamented, "The care of $200 million is too great a load for any brain or back to bear. It is enough to kill anyone. There is no pleasure in it."[25]

The words of Solomon, Rockefeller, and Vanderbilt should remind us that we will *never* find real contentment in chasing earthly riches. Do we need money? Sure. Is it wrong to have money? No. But *having* and *chasing* are two very different things. Our God, I'm happy to say, has a much better path for us to follow.

In Search of True Contentment

Satan is a crook, a liar, and a thief, but he's a smart crook, liar, and thief. He knows us well and he has an all-too-effective plan to tempt us into believing that our level of happiness and contentment depends on the size of things like our bank account, house, and garage.

In our search for contentment, Satan wants us to focus on anything but God. His strategy for setting up a stronghold of greed and materialism within our hearts includes a campaign to convince us that the more we have, the happier we'll be. It's a simple strategy, really. But he's found it staggeringly effective, both in the world and among too many Christians.

The devil doesn't want us to focus *on* something so much as he wants to take our focus *off* of something else. He'll do whatever he can to make us blind to the life of contentment we enjoy when we focus fully on Jesus Christ.

In 1 Timothy 6:6, Paul revealed that he isn't against gain, but against useless gain: "Godliness with contentment is great gain," he said. He wasn't against investment, but against bad investment. The word "contentment" in this verse connotes being unmoved or unaffected by external circumstances. It means being so content and satisfied that you feel no need to seek out more than God provides.

This is the kind of contentment reflected in the ancient prayer of a man named Agur: "Remove falsehood and lies far from me; give me neither poverty nor riches—feed me with the food allotted to me; lest I be full and deny You, and say, 'Who is the LORD?' or lest I be poor and steal, and profane the name of my God" (Proverbs 30:8-9).

Paul told Timothy, "We brought nothing into this world, and it is certain we can carry nothing out. And having food and clothing, with these we shall be content" (1 Timothy 6:7-8).

Something about being content with God's provision creates within us a grateful heart. I believe that one of the keys for avoiding the stronghold Paul calls "the love of money" is remembering with a grateful heart everything God so lovingly provides. Gratitude and contentment naturally push greed and materialism out of the human heart.

When did you last thank God for all of the blessings He has bestowed on you? When did you last take inventory of the many ways God provides for you, sustains you, protects you? If it's been a while, why not stop right now and take some time for an impromptu worship service? I'd call that a fantastic strategy to begin taking down any stronghold of greed that might be going up in your heart.

Generous Giving: Antidote for Greed

Ron Blue, a Christian author with more than forty years of experience in financial services, has written more than fifteen books on personal finance, all from a biblical perspective. In an article on his website, titled "The Antidote for Materialism" and written by one of the advisors in his company, I saw a thought that nearly made me jump out of my seat and shout "Amen!"

"Giving is an effective antidote to materialism."[26]

I've concluded that any Christian who chooses to give generously and with a joyful heart is a Christian who won't struggle with the love of money. The stingy Christian, on the other hand, will continue to love money (and be enslaved by it).

The apostle Paul offered a potent stronghold-busting principle that works as well in our age as it did in the first century: "Command those who are rich in this present age not to be haughty, nor to trust in uncertain riches but in the living God, who gives us richly all things to enjoy. Let them do good, that they be rich in good works, ready to give, willing to share, storing up for themselves a good foundation for the time to come, that they may lay hold on eternal life" (1 Timothy 6:17-19).

I love the phrase "ready to give, willing to share," because it depicts a person who has purposed in his heart to give generously and not out of some constrained sense of mere duty. This is a person who takes the Word of God seriously when it says, "So let each one give as he purposes in his heart, not grudgingly or of necessity; for God loves a cheerful giver" (2 Corinthians 9:7).

Strongholds of materialism and greed are very hard to erect on the soil of generosity. While generosity provides a rock-solid foundation for a life of faith, it acts like quicksand for the construction of a stronghold. An open hand tends to knock down this stronghold's walls.

Two Kinds of Rich Men

A few years back, a well-to-do businessman called me and said he wanted to give a substantial gift to our ministry. "I just need to get with my CPA and my attorneys to get everything in order, and then I'll let you know when it's going to come," he said.

I remember hanging up the phone and shouting, "Praise the Lord!" I knew we could put the gift to good use for God's kingdom, and I started making tentative plans on how we would use it.

Good thing those plans were tentative.

I waited for weeks to hear back from this man, but the gift never arrived. One day he finally called me back and sheepishly said, "I guess you're wondering where the gift I promised is."

I sure am! I thought. But I listened as he explained: "Where the market's at right now, it's just not a good time." We talked for a bit longer, then said good-bye and hung up.

After the call I started thinking that maybe the man wasn't as smart in business as I had thought. My mind went toward some scriptural principles concerning giving, principles I think any of us should put into practice if we want God's best blessings (and if we want to avoid the stronghold of greed).

It occurred to me that this man seemed far more concerned about what his CPA and attorneys had said than about what God says about giving. King Solomon, the richest man in the world in his time, offered up some real wisdom on the subject: "There is one who scatters, yet increases more; and there is one who withholds more than is right, but it leads to poverty. The generous soul will be made rich, and he who waters will also be watered himself" (Proverbs 11:24-25).

Solomon meant that just as those who scatter more seed tend to reap a bigger crop, so the generous man's giving will make him richer. It's always been true: Stinginess tends to lead to poverty, while generous giving tends to generate more wealth (and not just in material things).

Am I saying that when you give generously, you should wait by your mailbox for a big check to arrive? Not at all! God may choose to reward you financially when you choose to give generously, and He often does; but if that happens, He does so in order that you can become even more generous in your giving. Never give with the expectation of receiving more financial riches! That in itself demonstrates a heart of greed, a soul that loves money.

God may instead bless you for your generosity with treasure that money can't buy. New friends? A greater sense of purpose? The opportunity to see lives healed, bettered, saved? These are the kinds of treasure Jesus talked about when He said, "Do not lay up for yourselves treasures on earth, where moth and rust destroy and where thieves break in and steal; but lay up for yourselves treasures in heaven, where neither moth nor rust destroys and where thieves do not break in and steal. For where your treasure is, there your heart will be also" (Matthew 6:19-21).

Paul wrote that the generous rich folk from Timothy's congregation could store "up for themselves a good foundation for the time to come, that they may lay hold on eternal life" (1 Timothy 6:19). These men, who had received financial blessings from God, could choose to use their money in a way that would, in effect, send their money ahead of them to heaven.

When you become a cheerful giver, you beat back the stronghold of greed. Giving reminds you that you are not the owner, but merely the steward of everything in your care. None of us actually owns any of the material blessings God gives us. God owns it all. We are just the temporary managers of all the money and material blessings that come our way.

Good stewards stand before God, asking Him to bless them, with hands open and stretched upward to receive from Him. But when they go out into their corners of the world, they put their hands out with palms down, looking for opportunities to bless others.

Jesus made this point beautifully when He told the parable of the rich fool (Luke 12:16-21). The rich man's land produced a bumper crop, but instead of giving away the excess to the needy, he decided to build larger barns so he could hoard his crops and "eat, drink, and be merry."

The miser didn't know that he was about to face God's judgment. "Fool! This night your soul will be required of you," God announced. "Then whose will those things be which you have provided?"

Jesus wanted to make two important points with this parable. First, God never intended that we devote ourselves to accumulating earthly riches. Second, He doesn't bless us materially so that we can spend it all on ourselves. On the contrary, He blesses us so that we can bless others and direct some of our assets toward building His eternal kingdom. Those who do that He calls "rich toward God" (verse 21).

Could you call yourself "rich toward God"? Don't wake up one morning to find that the money you spent on a new house actually went to build the foundation for a stronghold of greed.

Two Kinds of Rich Men

There are two kinds of rich men. The first kind hold on tightly to everything they have; the love of money has overtaken them. They build *really* big strongholds. Those in the second group understand that by sharing their earthly treasures with others, they are in fact storing up treasures for themselves in heaven. They love the Lord and the people around them, and they look ahead to the end results of their gifts. Strongholds of greed just can't nab any real estate in their lives.

Jesus told His followers, "Take heed and beware of covetousness, for one's life does not consist in the abundance of the things he possesses" (Luke 12:15). Those dominated by the love of money spend their time pursuing temporal things, even though all of them are locked into time and space. But those who love God and people see their material blessings as a means to expanding His eternal kingdom, and the good they do with their money follows them into the next life.

One is a great investment, the other is not. Which are you choosing?

9

Pride: The Devil's Sin

'   've had many chances over the years to offer advice to young professionals who ask me what they should do to have long, blessed careers. I usually tell them, "God could use you more if you could go lower."

Some of these young men are extremely talented, gifted, and highly motivated to make a difference in the world around them; but more than that, they feel a call to serve and to make a mark on God's eternal kingdom. So why do I tell them God could use them more if they would just go lower?

I want to warn them against letting human pride swoop in and ruin what could become something great. I don't want them to mess up their calling by letting a self-sufficient, ambitious, self-congratulatory spirit rule their hearts. Instead, I encourage them to make humility a hallmark of every part of their lives.

Adrian Rogers understood this as well or better than any man I've ever known. Adrian wasn't even twenty years old when he felt God's unmistakable call to preach. At the time he still lived in his hometown of West Palm Beach, Florida, and he felt God leading him to take an unusual but highly symbolic step of humility before he began what would become an incredible ministry.

He went out to a baseball field near his home, got on his knees in the dirt infield, and surrendered himself to the Lord. Somehow, though, he didn't feel that he had brought himself low enough before God. So he laid out across the ground, face down in the dirt, and committed himself to God. But still that didn't seem like enough. So he dug a hole in the dirt, stuck his nose in the hole, and again surrendered himself to the God who in time would make him one of the greatest (and yet most humble) Christian voices of the twentieth century.

God showed Adrian Rogers something early in his ministry about pride and humility that far too many men don't learn until much later. God wants us to know that while pride brings death, humility brings life. It saddens me to think about the terrible examples I've seen of men, even those called to do great things for God's kingdom, who allowed pride to build strongholds in their hearts. Those strongholds wrecked their careers...and sometimes their lives.

The Destructive Power of Pride

I believe that sex, greed, and pride are intertwined. Those really are the Big Three that take down most men. I also believe that pride may be the most dangerous of them all, because if you don't get right with God in the area of pride, you'll have a much more difficult time getting right with Him in the other two areas.

All three of these issues can create within a man a twisted sense of entitlement, which leads to sins and consequences beyond the original sin itself. For example, many a married man has justified an extramarital affair by telling himself, *My wife hasn't been treating me right, so I deserve this. If she'd take care of business at home, I wouldn't need to do this.* He thinks of himself (pridefully so) as "entitled" to the affair because he feels deprived. What he doesn't understand is that the sin of adultery will lead to all sorts of other sins: lying, financial impropriety, jealousy, and hatred and theft, which in turn generate damaged relationships, loss of residence, court dates, and even a job loss or civil lawsuits.

Sinful pride can cause men to engage in the same kind of rationalization regarding money. Greed and materialism also spring from a sense of entitlement, and that can take a man to a place where he'll do things he knows are wrong to acquire more money and possessions. Why? *Because I deserve it.*

But let me take this point a step further. I believe that pride is the common denominator of *all* sin. All sorts of sexual immorality and greed, as well as idolatry, covetousness, filthy talk, disobedience, gossip, hatred, anger, murder, and lying are all, in some way, rooted in sinful human pride.

Though pride is often a subtle, insidious sin, it is also breathtakingly dangerous. The Bible warns us, "Pride goes before destruction, and a haughty spirit before a fall" (Proverbs 16:18). The word translated "destruction" implies a total shattering of what a man has and is, along with everything he could have and could be. It's as though the prideful man has fallen to his death from a cliff.

Pride is also dangerous because it keeps people from seeking God. An unnamed psalmist wrote, "The wicked in his proud countenance does not seek God; God is in none of his thoughts" (Psalm 10:4). A proud, arrogant man is almost always a self-sufficient man, and a self-sufficient man can never acknowledge his own sin or his own need for God.

Pride can lead us to believe that we are strong enough in and of ourselves to resist the temptation to sin. The apostle Paul gave us a very direct warning against this kind of pride when he wrote to the Corinthian church about the sins of the Israelites during the time of the Exodus. He reminded his Christian friends how often God's chosen people had given into temptation and how dearly it cost so many of them. Then came the all-important takeaway: "Now all these things happened to them as examples, and they were written for our admonition, upon whom the ends of the ages have come. Therefore let him who thinks he stands take heed lest he fall" (1 Corinthians 10:11-12).

Let him who thinks he stands take heed lest he fall. This stark warning should remind us that every man has it within him to be unfaithful to God. We should take this as a challenge to live not in pride, but in dependency on God.

Sinful pride can cause any man, including a professing Christian, to think he's better than others. He may point to differences in socioeconomic status, education, or even spiritual maturity and say, "That proves I have God's favor. Maybe someday he'll catch up." Who among us hasn't driven through a poor neighborhood and thought, *I'm glad I don't live here around* these *people.* Or maybe we encountered someone we perceived as being less spiritual or educated and branded him a "lesser light."

Proud men display all kinds of sinful attitudes. Their arrogance keeps them from seeing that Jesus Christ died for every person they meet, including those who are less fortunate than themselves. Jesus told us He rewards those who choose to serve "the least of these" (Matthew 25:40), but how can we truly serve anyone when we see ourselves as better than them?

The Subtle Lure of Pride

I've heard it said that pride is the most insidious sin in all the world. As I've thought about the nature of pride and how it can so easily gain a stronghold in the life of any man, I'd have to agree.

The word *insidious* describes something that can cause harm but in a gradual, subtle, or altogether unnoticed way. That word really sums up the danger of sinful pride. What's worse is that the insidious nature of pride makes it easier for the devil to set up a devastating stronghold within from which to attack us.

Pride also has an immortal, relentless, zombie-like quality to it.

No matter how many times we kill it, it always seems to come back from the dead. It's like some slimy creature in an old B movie that the hero kills but which keeps coming back in another form. You can kill pride, drive a stake through its heart, burn it to a crisp, bury it, and then bury the shovel you used to dig the hole, but pride still comes back and tries to take another chunk out of your life.

A Closer Look at Pride

The apostle Paul once wrote to some dear Christian friends, "Great is my boldness of speech toward you, great is my boasting on your behalf. I am filled with comfort. I am exceedingly joyful in all our tribulation" (2 Corinthians 7:4). Another Bible version translates the phrase about boasting like this: "I take great pride in you" (NIV).

Although in the English language the word "pride" reads the same way in this context as it does in biblical verses that condemn sinful pride—"Pride and arrogance and the evil way and the perverse mouth I hate" (Proverbs 8:13)—the kind of pride Paul mentions in 2 Corinthians 7:4 is not the variety God repeatedly tells us He hates.

Paul has in mind the same kind of pride you might feel when you and your co-workers do a great job on a project, or the kind you might express to your son or daughter for an especially impressive report card, athletic achievement, or act of kindness. As the good folk from the Deep South might say, "Ain't nothin' wrong with that!"

On the other hand, sinful pride, as described in the Bible, refers to holding an exalted opinion of self, overconfidence in self, self-righteousness, arrogance, an attitude of superiority. It screams of self-reliance and not reliance on God. It pictures a heart and mind devoted to accomplishing one's own goals and not God's desires. It's giving oneself credit for what God has done.

Ain't nothin' good about *any* of that!

The word *pride* derives from a word meaning "high." It suggests the elevation of one's self so that he looks down on others. The biblical verb translated "humble," on the other hand, suggests the conscious lowering of one's self. It depicts a person who does not overvalue himself and as a result devalue those around him.

Ever had to spend time with someone filled with arrogant pride? Someone who constantly talks about himself in the most glowing ways possible, gives off an annoying air of superiority, seems overly concerned with making others think highly of him, and uses the words *I*, *me*, *my*, and *mine* more than any other in the English language?

When I meet someone like that, it usually doesn't take long to recognize him as a man with a major stronghold in his life. I know he needs God's grace so that he can become the humble man the Lord calls all of us to be—and so that he can avoid the consequences of his sinful pride. I feel a degree of compassion for him and I try to make it a point to pray for him.

At the same time, being around that kind of man usually makes me want to run for the nearest exit. It can be draining to hang around an overly prideful and arrogant person! Most of us would prefer to endure a root canal. I've spent time around humble men and I've spent time around prideful men, and I greatly prefer the company of the humble.

But this should cause us to think. If we fallen, sinful human beings dislike the company of a prideful man, then how do you think a holy, perfect God feels about human pride? If you read what the Bible has to say on the subject, you know it's not good.

Consider just a few examples:

- "Everyone proud in heart is an abomination to the LORD; though they join forces, none will go unpunished" (Proverbs 16:5).

- "Do you see a man wise in his own eyes? There is more hope for a fool than for him" (Proverbs 26:12).

- "The pride of your heart has deceived you, you who dwell in the clefts of the rock, whose habitation is high; you who say in your heart, 'Who will bring me down to the ground?'" (Obadiah 1:3).

- "Whoever secretly slanders his neighbor, him I will destroy; the one who has a haughty look and a proud heart, him I will not endure" (Psalm 101:5).

The word "pride," or variations on it or synonyms for it, appears in the Bible dozens of times. If you study the passages in which the word appears, you'll see that almost never is it used positively. It nearly always appears in a context of sin and evil, which can suggest only one conclusion: God hates pride. In fact, the word *hates* probably doesn't do justice to God's view of pride.

The Bible declares, "These six things the LORD hates, yes, seven are an abomination to Him," and then goes on to list "a proud look" among these deadly sins (Proverbs 6:16-19). For comparison's sake, take a look at some of the other sins listed: lying, murder, a wicked heart. Pride is that bad? Yes, it's that bad.

Pride is a big part of our fallen nature, which I believe is why God addresses it so frequently in Scripture—and why He hates it so passionately.

With Pride Comes Shame

The Bible tells us that, "when pride comes, then comes shame; but with the humble is wisdom" (Proverbs 11:2). Quite a contrast, isn't it? It's also quite a choice for each of us. The God who hates pride more than any other human sin tells us that we can choose sinful human pride and the humiliation and shame it will surely bring us, or we can choose humility and wisdom and life.

But the Bible doesn't just *tell* us pride will bring people to shame; it *shows* us, through many real-life examples. Consider just a few:

Adam and Eve

Genesis 3 describes the rebellion of the first humans. It tells of the serpent—actually the devil in snake's clothing—appealing to human pride. "You will not surely die," he said to Eve. "For God knows that in the day you eat of it your eyes will be opened, and you will be like God, knowing good and evil" (verses 3-4).

Eve bought into the temptation of wanting to be like God (another extreme definition of the word *pride*), disobeyed her God, and Adam quickly followed. Sin then became a part of the human condition, and with it something neither of the first two humans had ever experienced: shame. Adam felt such intense shame over what he had done that he tried to hide himself from God. He didn't want his Creator, the One who designed him and shaped him and brought him to life, to see him naked. How does that even make sense? It doesn't. But that's what pride will do to you.

Uzziah

King Uzziah was one of the few good kings of Judah. He did some great things for his nation and served God faithfully for most of his fifty-two-year reign. Second Chronicles 26:5 tells us, "as long as he sought the LORD, God made him prosper." Sadly, though, all of his fame and power went to his head, and he sinned against God by entering the temple to burn incense on the altar—a service God had set aside for priests alone to do. Apparently Uzziah thought he had risen above all that; he was great enough to do it all for himself. When the priests confronted him about his sin, he flew into a rage. At that very moment, leprosy broke out on Uzziah's forehead, and he ended up spending the rest of his life isolated because of his disease (see 2 Chronicles 26:16-23).

Nebuchadnezzar

Considered the greatest monarch of ancient Babylon, King Nebuchadnezzar provides us with a perfect picture of sinful pride, as well as the consequences that accompany it. God used him to bring judgment on the nation of Judah for its idolatry and rebellion, and he rose to become the most powerful man on earth.

The Bible tells us that Nebuchadnezzar looked at everything he had built with overweening pride and self-satisfaction. He gazed over his magnificent city and said, "Is not this great Babylon, that I have built for a royal dwelling by my mighty power and for the honor of my majesty?" (Daniel 4:30). God doesn't tend to respond well to such speeches or such attitudes. Immediately the Lord humbled the king, causing him to go insane. Nebuchadnezzar spent seven years living like an animal, spending all his time in a field and eating grass, his hair and fingernails growing out of control.

C.S. Lewis rightly called pride "the complete anti-God state of mind."[27] He saw pride as competitive by nature, so that it takes no pleasure in good things, only in having more things or better things or more expensive things than someone else. He wrote,

> If you want to find out how proud you are the easiest way is to ask yourself, "How much do I dislike it when other people snub me, or refuse to take any notice of me, or shove their oar in, or patronise me, or show off?" The point is that each person's pride is in competition with everyone else's pride. It is because I wanted to be the big noise at the party that I am so annoyed at someone else being the big noise.[28]

What kind of results do you get when you take Lewis's test? How proud have you become, perhaps without realizing it?

Satan, the Ultimate Picture of Pride

I doubt we can have a complete, Bible-based discussion of sinful pride without considering the devil himself. The Bible describes Satan as a beautiful creation of God, a covering cherub, an angelic creature who lived with other created beings in heaven with God (Ezekiel 28:12-14).

But the devil, also called Lucifer, came to overflow with pride. His breathtaking beauty and his lofty status so filled him with arrogance that he attempted to take a position above that of God Himself (Isaiah 14:13-14). Remember how Lewis said pride is essentially competitive? Because of Lucifer's pride and arrogance, God permanently cast him out of heaven. Read what the prophet Isaiah wrote about this moment:

> How you are fallen from heaven,
> O Lucifer, son of the morning!
> *How* you are cut down to the ground,
> You who weakened the nations!
>   For you have said in your heart:
> "I will ascend into heaven,
> I will exalt my throne above the stars of God;
> I will also sit on the mount of the congregation
> On the farthest sides of the north;
> I will ascend above the heights of the clouds,
> I will be like the Most High" (Isaiah 14:12-14).

As you read the words of Isaiah, it's hard to miss how many times Lucifer uttered the word "I." His excessive use of that word is a sure sign of someone filled with pride. Although he's still fighting on today, doing his worst to trap humans in strongholds of pride, Satan will one day pay the ultimate price for his arrogance.

Here's the thing we all need to understand about our God: He is not just the Creator of all things, but He's also the sovereign Lord of all. He's not about to share His position or His glory with any created thing! He's not in competition with anyone, and never will be.

That, more than anything else, is why God hates pride and why He says He will always resist the proud.

God with You?

I once saw a T-shirt bearing the message, *"There is a God. You are not Him."* I love that! It is a reminder that we need to know our place in the big picture and to humbly remember that God is in charge—not us.

Pride leads us to believe that we're in charge, that we have to take care of things on our own. But the Bible tells us, "God opposes the proud, but gives grace to the humble" (James 4:6 ESV). The word translated "opposes" means more than that God passively stands back and lets the pride-filled man go his own way. It's more than simply allowing that man to reap the natural consequences of his sin. It's much more ominous than that! It means God has purposefully, willfully, and irreversibly set Himself against every proud person. And why does God hate pride so much? Read C.S. Lewis again:

> Pride...has been the chief cause of misery in every nation and every family since the world began. Other vices may sometimes bring people together: you may find good fellowship and jokes and friendliness among drunken people or unchaste people. But Pride always means enmity—it is enmity. And not only enmity between man and man, but enmity to God. In God you come up against something that is in every respect immeasurably superior to yourself. Unless you know God as that—and, therefore, know yourself as nothing in comparison—you do not know God at all. As long as you are proud you cannot know God. A proud man is always looking down on things and people: and, of course, as long as you are looking down, you cannot see something that is above you.[29]

Whether you're the CEO of a multinational corporation, the pastor of a world-famous megachurch, a powerful national political figure, or a community leader with deep pockets and impressive connections, God says clearly and repeatedly in His Word that if you are filled with sinful human pride, then He's not on your side. In fact, He's against you.

That alone should scare us humble!

The thought that God could ever be against me because of my pride overwhelms me. I can't imagine stepping up to the pulpit on Sunday morning knowing that, though the congregation might be with me, God is against me.

The apostle Paul instructed some Christian friends, "Let nothing be done through selfish ambition or conceit, but in lowliness of mind let each esteem others better than himself. Let each of you look out not only for his own interests, but also for the interests of others" (Philippians 2:3-4).

The man who consistently applies this verse to his life would present a good example of a humble servant, wouldn't he? But if you turn those words around, you'd have a spot-on example of a man with a heart filled with wicked pride: "Do everything through selfish ambition, and in highness of mind esteem yourself as better than others. Look out for your own interests first, not the interests of others."

Pride prompts a man to do everything with an eye toward his own benefit. It causes him to look down on others and to insist that they look up to him. It mars his every action, no matter how outwardly noble it may seem, with the expectation that he'll reap personal benefit from his work and that others will heap words of praise on him for all the "good" he does.

I know some of that lives in me. I've struggled with pride. And I know that if I allow the devil to use that stronghold to get me to "do everything through selfish ambition," I could lose it all tomorrow. And frankly, if that's how I began to act, I *should* lose it all.

I recently told someone, "We don't create waves. We just surf them." I'm just along for the ride, and I couldn't be more grateful to God for letting me in on what He's doing.

Choose Humility

Walking along the road of human pride always brings divine opposition. By contrast, the pathway to God's blessing and grace is paved with humility. Do you want to avoid divine opposition and receive divine grace? If so, you must make a conscious decision to humble yourself.

The apostle Peter, who learned some powerful lessons about humility during his time with Jesus, advised us to "humble yourselves under the mighty hand of God, that He may exalt you in due time" (1 Peter 5:6).

I've seen a lot of men crash and burn because of pride. The politician who wouldn't admit his mistake. The CEO who thought he was smarter than everyone else. The doctor who wouldn't listen to his colleagues. The factory worker who wanted to dominate his fellow workers. It never turns out well.

If you want something better for yourself, I suggest you pray something like this: "Lord, I humble myself before You. I submit myself to You and ask You to remind me daily that everything I do should be with the motive of glorifying You and only You."

This is a daily battle for me, as I imagine it is for many other Christian men. But when we repent of our sinful pride and replace it with godly humility, we can say with confidence, "If God is for us, who can be against us?" (Romans 8:31).

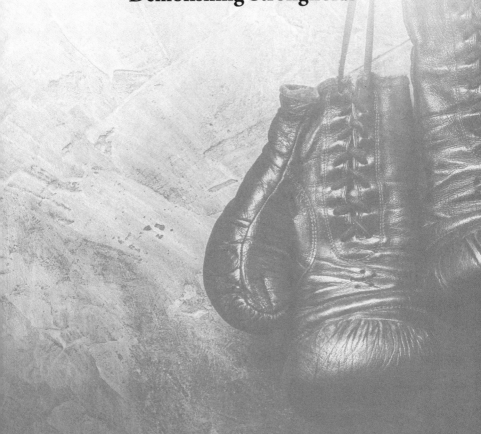

Part Three

Invincible Weapons for Demolishing Strongholds

10

Weapon 1: Confess and Repent

We've been holding men's conferences at Woodstock Church for a quarter of a century. Over that time, I've heard all kinds of stories from men around the country about the strongholds that have kept them bound for months, years, and even decades. The vulnerability of these men always amazes me as they describe their past and how they're finally winning their freedom.

One man told me he's struggled with pornography since he was four years old. *Good night!* I thought. Others have told me similar stories, describing the crippling strongholds that have devastated them since they were seven, or nine, or eleven years old. To a man they've told me something like this: "I always feared what people would think if I told anyone. But in getting this out in the open, I've been embraced by the love of God. Man, it feels so *good* just to be free!"

And I think, *Dear God, why would any man not want to be free? Why would anyone not want to feel clean on the inside?* How can you worship God and know that when you lift your hands, your hands actually aren't clean? I say this with all the compassion in my heart:

You *must* do whatever it takes to get yourself to the place where you're enjoying unhindered peace and joy. You must change whatever needs to change in your life so that you can live with no regrets, no retreat, and no reserve.

One thing is for sure: Nothing will change unless you choose to admit your problem and then do an about-face. The Bible calls this process confession and repentance—these are the necessary first steps toward demolishing the strongholds that have taken control of your life.

Sin: An Offense Against God

Before we look at the restoring power of confession and repentance, I think we should consider why sin is such a big deal in the first place. Why is it so important that we refuse to tolerate failure in our struggles with sin? The primary reason is that sin is offensive *to God*.

Many of us struggle with our attitude toward sin because we are naturally more self-centered than God-centered. We are more concerned about our victory over sin than we are that our sin grieves the heart of God.

I've dealt with men who got caught in sin, but who just got angry at themselves. They felt upset because they had fallen, but they never saw their sin as an offense against God. This self-centered focus, instead of a God-centered focus, set them up for another fall later on.

One of our lead Bible study teachers at Woodstock called me one day. He seemed to have about as good a grasp on the Word of God as any Sunday school teacher we had. "One passage has always confused me," he said. "Can you shed any light on it? It's found in Psalm 51, where David said, 'Against You, You only, have I sinned.' How could David say he had sinned against God only when he had arranged to have Uriah killed? He had also committed adultery with Bathsheba. He had sinned against both of them as well."

"No, he didn't," I replied. "Bathsheba never came up with a law that said it is a sin to commit adultery. I don't read in my Bible where

Uriah said murder is a sin. *God* said murder is a sin. *God* called adultery a sin. Every time you sin, it's an offense against God. It may involve someone else and hurt someone else, but the real sin is always against God."

Until we begin to grasp that our sin offends God—and that this is the real problem—we will never gain victory over sin.

William S. Plumer, a highly regarded Bible teacher in the 1800s, wrote,

> We never see sin aright until we see it as against God...All sin is against God in this sense: that it is His law that is broken, His authority that is despised, His government that is set at naught...Pharaoh and Balaam, Saul, and Judas each said, "I have sinned"; but the returning prodigal said, "I have sinned against heaven and before thee"; and David said, "Against Thee, Thee only have I sinned." [30]

There are those who feel remorseful for their actions, but their remorse leaves them unchanged. Then there are those who, like David, feel remorse for their sin *and* see it as an offense against God. That insight drove David to confess his sin, turn from it, find forgiveness, and set out again on a path that pleased God and filled the repentant king with joy.

Confession: Saying What God Says

After the prophet Nathan confronted David about his sin, the king confessed. He said immediately, "I have sinned." He could have said, "Nathan, old buddy, do you not understand what happened? I mean, Bathsheba was out there *naked*, under the full moon. Nude! Dear God, how can a red-blooded man keep his desires under control with the way women dress these days?"

When a man holds back the truth about his sin or tells you only part of it, he is not repentant. Possibly remorseful, but not repentant.

A lot of people feel sorry they got caught. They weep because of the loss that's coming because they got caught—but they're not repenting.

David said to God, "Against You...have I sinned, and done this evil in your sight" (Psalm 51:4). He spelled it out. He didn't claim that he had made an unfortunate mistake, or unintentionally messed up, or done only what everybody else was doing. He said, "I have done evil."

To confess means that you agree with God, that you call sin what God calls it. When you genuinely repent of your sin, there are three things you won't do: First, you won't minimize your sin. Second, you won't rationalize your sin. And third, you won't generalize your sin; in fact, you'll explicitly and specifically confess exactly what you did. You won't say something generic like, "Please forgive me for whatever wrong I may have done."

Confession puts it all out there—like an open book. You agree with God: "Here's what I've done wrong." If you need someone to forgive you, you tell them. You also tell someone who can help hold you accountable in the future because you want to move forward. If you want to truly experience God's forgiveness, you need the help of those around you who love you, who believe you're trying to get back on the right track. You have to be honest and open with them (more on this in chapter 14).

Sometime after author and former pastor Gordon MacDonald confessed to having an adulterous relationship, James Dobson interviewed him on air for one hour. Dobson asked if Gordon's wife asked him pretty explicit details about his affair.

"She sure did," he replied.

Dobson went on to say that Gordon owed it to her to tell her the truth because he deceived her in his immoral act.

After David finally confessed his adulterous relationship, he wrote, "When I kept silent, my bones grew old through my groaning all the day long" (Psalm 32:3). So long as he told no one what he had done, it felt as though he were wasting away, as if his very bones were disintegrating inside of him. God knew of his sin, of course, which is why David could pray, "Day and night Your hand was heavy upon me" (verse 4).

When you sin against God, the Holy Spirit will keep His hand on you day and night until you admit whatever you've done. David wrote, "My vitality was turned into the drought of summer" (verse 4). In the language of the prophet Jeremiah, the king had morphed from a lush, green tree by the bank of a flowing river into a dry, brown bush in the blistering desert. He'd completely lost his victory.

That all changed the moment David finally confessed. "I acknowledged my sin to You, and my iniquity I have not hidden," he wrote. "I said, 'I will confess my transgressions [where he'd stepped across the line] to the LORD'" (verse 5). David finally reached the point in his life where he said, "I just can't keep silent any longer."

Always deal honestly with the Lord. Tell Him exactly how you feel: "God, I'm struggling. In fact, I confess that I didn't even want to pray right now. But I'm having some real struggles, and Lord, You know my heart. Everything in my flesh wants to say yes, but I pray the Spirit of God would give me a way of escape."

A lot of men end up having to confess their sin when they could have avoided it altogether. God always provides a way of escape from every temptation we ever face, even if it's just a narrow passageway. No man can ever honestly say, "I just didn't have a choice. I got in over my head and there was no way out."

In Jesus' name, there *is* a way out. Always! God never fails to provide the way of escape. When we fail to take advantage of that way, however, we need to own up to our sin and confess to God and others exactly what we did.

Cleansing: Forsaking the Sin

Forsaking sin follows confession of sin. We must decide to make a complete break from the sin and burn all bridges to it. To repent means to turn around and head in the other direction. Proverbs 28:13 says, "He who covers his sin will not prosper, but whosoever confesses *and forsakes them* will have mercy." If you want God's mercy, you have to reject the sin.

We once dealt with a married man who had committed adultery. When we tried to hold him accountable, we discovered that he had dropped by the woman's house to see her.

"What in the world are you doing?" we asked. "You should stay far away from there! Aren't you trying to be loyal to your wife?"

"Well, I can't just drop her," he said. "I mean, I care for the woman."

Yes, he *could* drop her. He was rationalizing his behavior. Until he was willing to truly forsake the sin, he was still hooked. He was still in bondage.

Men often say, "I want you to know I committed a sin. But I've repented." Well, whether that repentance is real or not will become evident in time. When a man genuinely repents, his life will give open, public testimony that he's repented. Time will tell.

When I first got saved, people who knew me said, "He'll get over it." They said this because so many who claim to get saved *do* get over it. For a little while they show a few signs of change, but eventually they go back to their old way of life. Do you know the only thing that will prove such skeptics wrong? When we *don't* get over it. And sometimes it takes a good bit of time for that to happen.

The bottom line is that if you say, "I have repented," your life must display what you state with your words. Make a clean and complete break from the sin and don't imagine you can handle it. It's never wise to overestimate your power to resist temptation!

When a dad wouldn't let his son stay out past midnight with his girlfriend, the young man got angry. "Don't you trust me, Dad?" the son demanded.

"No, I don't," replied the father. "I wouldn't trust *me* in that situation, so why in the world would I trust *you?*" A certain amount of self-distrust can help in the cleansing phase of repentance.

Contrition: Broken over Sin

True repentance involves a genuine brokenness over your sin. There's no defensiveness. You don't get angry. You're not proud. You're not bitter. You take full blame and full responsibility for what you did. Psalm 51:17 says, "The sacrifices of God are a broken spirit, a broken and a contrite heart—these, O God, You will not despise."

A contrite heart makes no demands and has no expectations. Broken and humble people are simply grateful to be alive. A man with a contrite heart does not place the blame on others. Instead, he will take the blame himself.

It would be easy to say after an affair, "This woman pursued me like a hound. Everywhere I turned, she was constantly pressing me." Statements like these, however, prove nothing except that you don't feel broken at all over your sin. And they accomplish nothing except to show that you haven't truly repented.

What if you have uncontrolled passions with no check in your spirit, and you never feel an inward conviction over doing wrong? Then I have to ask, "Are you sure you're in Christ? Are you sure Christ is in you?" No true believer can sin and be happy about it. You can't sin and not feel disturbed. Either you've learned to fake it or you are a fake.

Do you know one way I know that Christ lives in me? I can't sin and get away with it. He gets me every time. The One who matters most in the universe to me has shown me my fault—not to pick on me, but because He loves me and desires what's best for me. He convicts me, but He doesn't condemn me. Do you know the difference?

Conviction reminds me of who I really am and warns me that I'm not acting in line with my true identity in Christ. Conviction comes out of Christ's compassionate love for me. Condemnation, by contrast, comes from the devil and tells me that I'm rotten to the core, that I deserve hell, and that in fact I'm on the way there right now. When you sin and feel convicted to repent, that's God. When you sin and feel hopeless and condemned, that's Satan. Don't allow the enemy to trap you in a dark and miserable stronghold.

Claiming: Seeking Forgiveness and Reinstatement

When we repent of our sin and seek a fresh start, it's crucial that we claim God's forgiveness and expect reinstatement. When you claim God's grace, you gain the power, the ability, and the divine enablement to go on. Some people claim that they're repentant, but their lives do not show it—and they do not go on.

"Earth has no sorrows that heaven cannot heal," goes one of my favorite quotes. When David finally acknowledged his sin, confessed it, and turned from it, he could gladly say to God, "You forgave the iniquity of my sin" (Psalm 32:5). Centuries later, in a letter addressed to Christians, the apostle John wrote, "If we confess our sins, He is faithful and just to forgive us *our* sins and to cleanse us from all unrighteousness" (1 John 1:9).

Have you confessed your sin to God? Have you forsaken it? Has the recognition of your sin broken your proud spirit? That's all wonderful, but for real healing to take place, you have to experience God's grace. Ask the Lord to forgive you and cleanse you from *all* unrighteousness. He will!

The Results of Repentance

Some church observers have referred to *repentance* as the forgotten word in preaching. I personally believe that when real repentance takes place, changes will occur in three major areas.

First, you'll see a change in the desires of your heart. Before, you didn't care at all about the things of God; but now, you're consumed with a passion to please your Lord. You were a selfish, stingy individual, but God got hold of your heart. He put a desire in the depths of your soul to love Him and to love others.

Second, you'll see a change in the direction of your life. Before, you spent your life always going where *you* wanted to go, often to your own detriment. Now you long to spend your whole life walking in the direction that you believe God wants you to go.

Third, you'll see a change in the destiny of your soul. You're no longer going where you once were headed. You were bound for hell; now Jesus is taking you to heaven. And even here on earth, you behave more and more like a committed citizen of God's eternal kingdom.

Every once in a while, a man who needs to repent of some sin or other will say to me, "Johnny, I don't have to repent." I never argue with him. Instead, I go a step further. "You *can't* repent," I'll say. "It takes a man of God to allow the Lord Jesus Christ to humble him, to admit his fault, and to forsake it."

Do you want to be a man of God? Then humble yourself, admit your fault, turn from it, and accept the forgiveness of Jesus. And then, by God's grace, expect full reinstatement.

Confrontation: Help Your Brother Get Free

In all my years of ministry, only one man has ever come to me about his moral failure before his sin became known. All the others were exposed first and then had to be confronted. If we care about our brothers, we'll do what we can to help them win their freedom.

Jesus tells us that if we see a brother sin, we are to rebuke him. If he repents, we are to forgive him (see Luke 17:3). I believe there are four guidelines we need to keep in mind as we prepare to confront, in love, a brother who is caught in sin.

1. Know the truth.

Every now and then people will come to me about a person they think needs to be confronted. "Preacher," they say, "you need to get involved. You need to deal with this." I feel no urgency to respond to those situations. If I believe God wants me to be involved in some confrontation, I can seek His face. He will initiate it. He will tell me what to say. He will get me the truth about the matter. He will tell me when to do it and how to do it.

Only when you know the truth about a man's situation can you say to him, "Brother, you need to come clean. You need to be accountable. We need to work through this situation together so God can get you back on the road of living for Him."

2. Know the right timing.

A family called me one day and said, "We want you to go visit so-and-so. You need to go see him *today* and tell him he's sinned. Listen, you hold the Bible up in the pulpit and say you believe it—so you'd better get over there and visit him today." I didn't go. In fact, I haven't been yet. I didn't act like their little errand boy and jump right to their timing. They didn't know that I had already confronted the man on more than one occasion.

3. Know how to treat the man.

I don't confront a man just to mess him up. I approach him graciously. Proverbs 25:11-12 says, "A word fitly spoken is like apples of gold in settings of silver. Like an earring of gold and an ornament of fine gold is a wise rebuker to an obedient ear." God never called me to be ugly. The only person I want to be ugly toward is the devil.

4. Know the testimonies of confrontation.

Read testimonies of how God has used people like Nathan to confront unrepentant believers, and how those confrontations worked for good as the guilty men repented and came to know the forgiveness of God. Don't fear the loss of a friendship! If a man is genuinely your friend, you can confront him. God honors the truth, and only the truth sets people free. Lies keep people in bondage.

I know we all tend to shy away from telling people hard truth. We'd rather say, "No, I'll just be his friend." But a real friend will speak the truth. As we've seen, the Bible says, "He who covers his sins will not prosper" (Proverbs 28:13). If you want your friend to prosper, you'll choose to confront him in love and with a view toward restoration.

A while ago I pleaded with a young student at Southeastern Baptist Theological Seminary to get professional counseling. He left his three precious daughters and should return to them, but I can't persuade him to give me an ear. And yet I still need to speak the truth in love.

How can I say that I believe the Bible is the Word of God and that I believe God's truth sets us free, but still refuse to live in the world of truth? How can any Christian tell a man who's compromised his wedding vows, "You can't tell your wife the truth; it'll destroy your marriage"? If a marriage can't be built on truth, then what, in Jesus' name, *can* it be built on?

Someone called me one day to describe a persistent problem that had its roots in deception. The sin might have gone on for as long as twenty years. He asked me, "What can I do?"

"There is but one way to experience victory," I told him. "Tell the truth."

"Oh, but that's going to hurt them!" he replied.

"No," I insisted, "it'll set them free."

A day or two later, my phone rang at 1:35 a.m. I heard the excited voice of the person I'd spoken to, saying, "They're free, free, free!" And I thought, *Who has been counseling them all these years? Why don't we counsel people to tell the truth?*

Without a doubt, it often feels more convenient to lie or keep quiet than to tell the truth. But you and I have to be men. Did you know the Bible says that God desires truth in the inward parts (Psalm 51:6)? How can we consider ourselves men of God, living a life of integrity, if we won't even tell the truth?

We must be willing to tell the truth—to say, "I struggle with some of these issues too. Let's work through this together." If we argue and fuss a little, that's okay, so long as we work through it. I may have to say, "I'm sorry. I didn't say it to hurt you. I love and care about you deeply."

Very often you'll hear in reply, "Well, I love and care about you too." Despite the pain, or perhaps because of it, telling the truth can lead to greater intimacy.

Can the truth hurt? Yes, but that's all right. "Faithful are the wounds of a friend, but the kisses of an enemy are deceitful" (Proverbs 27:6). Tell the truth!

Let God Change You

Maybe you've reached the point where you're saying, "I just have to repent. I have to ask God to forgive me. I need my heart's desires changed. I need my life's direction changed. I need to make a fresh commitment to Jesus Christ."

Take a moment and tell God right now. Confess to God exactly how you've sinned and done evil in His sight. He already knows it, but He loves to hear you admit it so that you stop denying it or hiding it. Otherwise, He can't free you of it. Ask God to forgive you and to empower you to forsake that sin.

Some Bible scholars say there is one phrase that changes the whole story of the prodigal son: "He came to himself" (Luke 15:17). The prodigal finally began to think. He had not been thinking, but as he sat there in the hog pen, asking for scraps from the tables or to be allowed to eat pig slop, he finally started thinking.

"You know what?" he said to himself. "I have a good memory. I used to live with my daddy. He took good care of me. What am I doing *here*, in the far country?" That's when he began to say, "I'd rather be a slave in my daddy's house than live here anymore." That shows growth in humility.

It takes humility to come home. Pride won't let you come home. *What will people think of me?* When you humble yourself, you no longer care what people think of you. You just want to go home.

Are you living in the far country in your heart, in your soul, in your mind, in your life, in your family, in your work, in your finances? Are you in the far country? If you are, I urge you in the name of Jesus to come home.

You can fall in love with the far country, but when you begin to see it like Jesus sees it, the far country stinks. It no longer looks so good. It hurts to think about where you are—and all you want to do is come home.

God can change you. He changed me, and He's still changing me. He wants to do a work in your heart too. So come home. Let God change you, and live the rest of your life with no regret, no retreat, no reserve.

11

Weapon 2: Learn to Receive and Give Forgiveness

At a tremendously difficult time in my life, things got so dark that I told friends something inside of me had died. I had a real fear that the light would never come back on. I struggled with shame and guilt, because I helped to make my condition worse by never slowing down and instead, trying to keep going all the time.

It got so dark that I doubted I had a future. I'd lost my confidence and I thought, *What am I going to do? I'll see how long I can live off retirement and then in, who knows, maybe two years, things will be better. Maybe then I will get involved in itinerant ministry, just do men's conferences, or share my story.*

But God had different ideas. Through the power of forgiveness, He brought me back. Today I'm enjoying life and ministry as much or more than I ever have. I know there's hope for the hopeless. The light can shine again! I've discovered that forgiveness is an armor-piercing shell that no stronghold can survive.

When we remain in a state of unforgiveness, we hurt both ourselves and those around us. Each of us needs to receive God's forgiveness for ourselves, and then extend forgiveness to others—and often, that means forgiving ourselves.

There's Hope for You

No one ever needs to think, *There's no hope for me. I've gone too far.* And no Christian ever needs to think, *I may be forgiven, but I'm ruined.* The power of forgiveness can reach you wherever you are.

Someone may say to me, "You can run around and say, 'God forgave me' all you want to, but I'll never forgive you." Well, Jesus is my hiding place. He will preserve me from trouble and surround me with songs of deliverance (see Psalm 32:7). God's Word trumps the word of anyone else! Human speculation is no match for divine revelation. So let the water of God's Word wash over your soul, trumping anything that others may say. The world has all kinds of voices, but let His be the loudest in your ears. Listen to His roars instead of the shouting of others.

When we come to Christ through forgiveness, He frees us from guilt and restores us to the Father. God brings healing. The depression can lift. The emotional pain can dissipate. Our spirits and bodies can be renewed. Do you know it's been estimated that more than 80 percent of all illnesses today may be psychosomatic in origin? One medical doctor in our church constantly sends people to our counseling services because she believes their issues are more spiritual than medical.

God desires not only to forgive you of your sin, He wants you to live with the sense of being cleansed and whole again. He wants to redeem your life from destruction. He intervenes when you are hell-bent and ruining your own life. God sovereignly and providentially stops you in your tracks and as a result, renews your life.

Satan will often try to use your troubles to worry and weaken you, but God wants to use the same troubles to strengthen you. What the old preacher Alexander Maclaren said long ago remains true today: "God's kiss of forgiveness sucks the poison out of the wound."[31]

In Psalm 40:3, a repentant David said, "He has put a new song in my mouth—praise to our God; many will see it and fear, and will trust in the LORD." This was a man who moments before had been describing his deep anguish. He moved from regret to rejoicing, from silence to singing. How? Through forgiveness. When your soul is clean, a new song erupts in your heart that you sing with gusto to God.

By contrast, unconfessed sin is a horrible burden to carry. God loves you too much to allow unconfessed sin to remain in your life! He gives you every opportunity, every open door, to come clean. I'm glad that the hand that disciplines is the same hand that forgives and protects. God is personally drawing you to Himself so that you can become a partaker of His character. He wants you to be like Him. Through forgiveness, He can get vile things out of your life, knock hurtful things away from your soul, and fill your days with truth and beauty.

If your heart is grateful for receiving God's forgiveness, then you will be gracious in extending it to others…and to yourself.

I Can't Forgive Myself

Christian songwriter Matthew West wrote a song called "Forgiveness," which is based on the story of a woman whose daughter died in an accident caused by a reckless driver. The young man went to prison for vehicular homicide. Meanwhile, the lady went on a rampage against reckless and drunk drivers.

But one day she realized she needed to deal with her bitterness toward the man who took her daughter's life. Over time, the Lord helped her to forgive the guilty man. She eventually visited the prison and asked to see him. She walked into his holding cell and said, "I'm here to forgive you."

He broke down, weeping. He then said he didn't know how she could forgive him—he couldn't even forgive himself. She could do so, she explained, because the Lord had forgiven her. Colossians 3:13

had captured her heart: "As the Lord has forgiven you, so you also must forgive" (ESV).

Maybe you're a Christian and you've blown it big time. Have you been able to forgive yourself? If not, you're still in prison. You've allowed yourself to stay behind the razor fence, even though the prison door's open and the warden has announced, "You've served your sentence." Yet you've chosen to stay back there and drag your burdensome ball and chain around.

Why?

A Bad Place to Be Stuck

I have met so many men who have said, "Please pray for me. I just can't forgive myself." They're stuck. They may be great at forgiving others, but they can't forgive themselves. Or maybe they treat themselves like they treat others. Someone hurts them, and they never forgive the person. They mark the guy and go on without him. Either way, they're stuck.

Could that be you? You're not willing to forgive yourself and you're stuck. What a terrible place to be! Who wants to go to church Sunday after Sunday, only to be reminded that you're stuck? How can you experience God's forgiveness and then be willing to forgive yourself?

I'm convinced that the struggle against self-forgiveness is, in fact, a symptom of a deeper heart issue. That struggle is usually based upon two related things: ignorance of the truth, and an unwillingness to see yourself as God sees you.

If you're a Christian and you've done something awful for which you can't forgive yourself, then almost certainly you have an improper view of yourself. You need to see that God doesn't view you the way you're viewing yourself.

I can understand how you might have gotten to this dark place, however. At the heart of the Christian faith stand two great truths that many of us often have a hard time putting together.

Two Great Realities

All believers are caught in a tension between two massive realities, one negative and the other positive. They're both true, and they're both true at the same time. But very often, we tend to emphasize one over the other, or highlight one and forget the other. Before you continue with this chapter, I'd like you to spend some time pondering both realities:

1. We are fallen people, desperately in need of grace.

2. God loves us deeply and accepts us in Christ.

The first reality tells us that something has gone radically wrong with each of us. We are not as God originally created us to be. We fell for the devil's lie and ever since, we quite easily choose evil over good, self over others, wrong over right. We cannot put ourselves right. We need God to rescue us—not because we deserve it (we don't), but because otherwise we're toast.

On the other hand, the Bible makes it abundantly clear that God loves us. He isn't willing that we should stay in our wretched state. He sent His Son, Jesus Christ, to die for our sins so that when we put our faith in Him, He can accept us as though we were Jesus Himself.

Although we often have a hard time putting these two realities together, perhaps we can get a glimpse of how they mesh by considering what happens inside our own families. When my children did wrong as they were growing up, I voiced my disapproval of their actions and corrected them, but I always did so in love and for their good. I wanted to restore our family harmony. God does the same thing. When you sin, God doesn't cease to love you or refuse to accept you any longer. You are still His child, although He may have to discipline you to bring you back into full fellowship.

When we fail to embrace both realities on a heart level—when we minimize either truth: first, that we are fallen, or second, that God loves us and accepts us in Christ—it manifests itself in a variety of ways. Maybe you'll recognize yourself in what I'm about to describe.

Three Distortions

Those who refuse to forgive themselves suffer from at least one of three distortions, all based on what we could call prideful assumption. These three distortions interlock and often feed on one another. The end result is that they keep believers from living free, primarily by convincing them, "I have a right to be my own lawgiver and judge. I cannot let God be the lawgiver or allow Him to make His own judgment."

Any of these three distortions can ensnare a man, render him ineffective, and steal God's glory. They work together to keep men from forgiving themselves. Men trapped by these distortions base their behavior on what *they* think (instead of what God thinks) and on how *they* view themselves (instead of how God views them).

Do you see yourself in any of the following three distortions?

1. Overt Pride

A man duped by overt pride believes that he doesn't need God's grace; he thinks he can make it on his own. Failure to embrace the first reality—that he's fallen and in need of God's grace—deceives him. Overt pride keeps him from seeing that he needs the gift of God's grace.

2. Performance Trap

A man caught in the performance trap believes he *shouldn't* need God's grace. "I should be able to make it on my own," he says. "I shouldn't have to ask God to help me every time I turn around." The performance trap convinces a man that Christ's work is incomplete. He thinks, *While the death of Jesus gets me into heaven, I must earn the Father's love and acceptance.* This quest to make it apart from God sets him on a path of trying to find another way. He feels guilty, and so he can't forgive himself.

He lives in a horrible place that is made worse because he remembers where he used to be. He doesn't think he will ever be like he once was. He doubts he will ever be free again. He feels overwhelming guilt because he has to take responsibility for the awful thing he did. He knows he should never have done it. He feels crushing shame. It's killing him on the inside.

3. Self-Hatred

A man suffering from self-hatred says, "I just hate myself for what I did." We could call this "reverse pride." This man says, "I've blown it too badly. So I'm beyond God's grace."

Failure to embrace the second reality—that God deeply loves him and accepts him in Christ—leads to the sin of self-hatred. This sin, in effect, reinstates the condemnation from which Christ had already set him free. Although Jesus says there's no condemnation, this man says to God, "I don't care what You say. I have to reinstate the condemnation." He's trying to trump God, to establish a standard higher than God's.

These three distortions work together to keep you from truly embracing God's love and acceptance. They prevent you from coming to a place of self-acceptance. Thank God there is a cure! But before we discuss it, let's look briefly at what God Himself has to say about your terrible predicament.

Is It True?

Start by reading the following passage. In your heart, do you agree or disagree that it expresses truth?

> If we say that we have no sin, we deceive ourselves, and the truth is not in us. If we confess our sins, He is faithful and just to forgive us our sins and to cleanse us of all unrighteousness (1 John 1:8-9).

Most theologians say that every verse of 1 John is written to

Christians. It's a book to the body of Christ. John insists that if any Christian says he has no sin, he deceives himself and the truth is not in him. But if that same Christian confesses his sins, God is faithful and just to forgive him those sins and to cleanse him of all unrighteousness.

Is that true?

The Bible also says that if you're a Christian, you don't belong to yourself anymore. "You are not your own…you were bought at a price," it declares, "therefore glorify God in your body and in your spirit, which are God's" (1 Corinthians 6:19-20).

God's Word says that you don't own yourself. God purchased you at the infinite cost of His dear Son's blood. God is therefore now Lord and owner of you, which means that *He's* the one who decides what's right and wrong, not you.

Is that true?

You may say, "Look, I see where you're going with this. But I don't deserve to be forgiven, and I guess that's why I'm not forgiving myself." Well, you're right that you don't deserve it. That's the marvelous thing about God's grace. It is *un*merited, *un*deserved. The first time you needed it to deal with your sin nature, you didn't deserve it. When you did something wrong after receiving salvation and you needed to experience God's grace, you still didn't deserve it. You *never* deserve it. If you did deserve it, it wouldn't be grace.

Read the following passage. Do you think it expresses truth?

> When we were still without strength, in due time Christ died for the ungodly. For scarcely for a righteous man will one die; yet perhaps for a good man someone would even dare to die. But God demonstrates His own love toward us, in that while we were still sinners, Christ died for us (Romans 5:6-8).

"Amazing Grace," the most popular hymn in the world, is all about verb tenses. Grace was applied in the past: "I *once* was lost, but *now* am found." Grace is being applied in the present: "'Tis grace hath brought me safe *thus far*." Grace will be applied in the future: "And grace *will* lead me home." I needed grace to get in, I need it now, and I'll need it to take me home. A life of faith begins in grace, continues by grace, and is consummated in grace. This is a great hymn not just because we like to sing it, but because the biblical theology of the song greatly honors God.

Do you think it's true?

Hold Up Your Head

In Psalm 3, we have an awesome record of the psalmist in trouble. He says, "Many are they who say of me, 'There's no help for him in God'" (verse 2). That's where you are when you reach the point of not forgiving yourself. You've not accepted yourself, and you're in deep trouble because of it. Maybe you've gotten used to hanging your head in shame. Although the psalmist knows what people are saying about him, he says, "You, O LORD, are a shield for me, my glory and the One who lifts up my head" (verse 3).

Whenever I visit the Maasai people in Uganda, if a boy approaches me as I'm standing there, he'll look down at the ground until I touch him on the head. That's the custom. When I reach down and touch him, he lifts his head.

You may feel worn down going to church because you feel shame. You can't lift your head. But when God accepts you because of Christ's sacrifice, it's as though God is reaching down and touching your head. God wants you to confess your feeling of shame and let Him set you free. He accepts you in Christ—not because of what you've done to come back to Him, but because of what He did so that you *could* come back to Him. He reaches down and touches you so you can lift your head.

God accepts you just as you are, with all your past, your present, and your future. He accepts you with whatever you brought from all the years before you came to Christ, to everything you bring now, to everything there will be by the time you die.

God doesn't divorce His people! Read the book of Hosea. You can go whoring like Gomer and God will come looking for you like Hosea. You can go down and sell yourself as a prostitute and He'll come and kick the hooker's stand from under you and take you home. That's the gospel. That is the God of the Bible. He loves you. You have a wrong view of Him.

You're accepted in the beloved. If the church puts you out, He doesn't. The church should never bring discipline except for one reason: restoration. That's why any fallen man would turn, come to his senses, cry out to God, and let the Lord lift his head.

In Psalm 3, we see how God begins to build boldness back into the life of a man who couldn't even lift his head, a man about whom the people were saying, "He has no hope." The psalmist said, "I will not be afraid of ten thousands of people who have set themselves against me all around" (verse 6). He's not being arrogant when he says that. His boast is in the Lord. His boast is in God's forgiveness. His boast is in the cross.

And his boast can be your boast.

Responding to the Distortions

Now let's look once more at the three distortions we considered earlier. How can a man free himself of them and walk once again in the love and acceptance of Jesus Christ?

1. Overt Pride

If you think, *I don't need God's grace; I can make it on my own,* you need to repent. True repentance—a change of mind in which you turn from sin to God—involves embracing reality as God defines it. When you refuse to forgive yourself, you're *not* embracing reality, because you're trying to live by what you define as true instead of what God defines as true. And what is God's truth? You are fallen and desperately in need of grace, yet God loves you deeply and accepts you completely in Christ.

Repent of the overt pride that tells you that you have a right to evaluate and judge your worth as a person. Only the Creator and Savior has that right! You and I have no such right. *Christ* judges sin. You must receive His forgiveness, not manufacture your own.

2. Performance Trap

Do you imagine you shouldn't need God's grace? But all of us do! You must come to accept that no man can make it on his own.

When Jesus died on the cross, He said, "It is finished, paid in full." He didn't say, "Well, all except for some stuff you have to work out on your own." Meditate upon the cross to the point where you start feeling a heartfelt gratitude for Christ's complete, finished work.

3. Self-hatred

Do you think you've done something so horrible that it's beyond God's grace? Impossible. God will accept anything if you bring it to Jesus. To say that He won't is to say that your sin is bigger than Jesus' sacrifice. What are you thinking? If you are saved, remember that there is *no* condemnation to those who are in Christ Jesus (Romans 8:1).

Meditate on the love of the Father, who freely gave you His Son. Thank Him for His love, mercy, and grace. You may need to say to Him, "I have no right to hate the one You love. I receive Your love."

Self-hatred was the problem of the prodigal son. When he "came to himself" and realized that even the lowest slaves on his father's estate were living better than he was, he determined to go home. He rehearsed a speech chock full of self-loathing: "I am no longer worthy to be called your son" (Luke 15:19). But what right did he have to set a standard higher than his father's? Was that his call?

More to the point, is it your call?

"I'll go to church, even though I don't deserve to be there. I'm not one of the family. I've blown it and I'll never be considered a son anymore. At best, put me down as a hired servant."

If you're saying that, you've listened to the devil, who's told you, "You shouldn't forgive yourself, you no-good, low-down servant. You're no son of God! Just look at how you've acted."

But when the prodigal son came home, his father didn't even let him recite his self-condemning speech. He never referred to his son as a servant, because he wasn't a servant; he was a son.

God's standards are higher than yours, so quit treating yourself as less than what God considers you. Start seeing yourself the way the Father sees you. If the Lord calls you a son, lift your head up. Step out of prison and slam the door behind you. Walk free!

Surrender to God's Love

Men who find it hard to forgive themselves are in fact struggling with *receiving* and *embracing* the gift of God's forgiveness, love, and acceptance. You may say, "Oh, I wish I could experience God's forgiveness." You can! Your continual self-condemnation and self-punishment reveals that you have set your own standard, evaluated your behavior, and have pronounced your own verdict: unforgiven.

Quit that! And surrender to the love of God.

Remember that in the Bible, the lawgiver is the forgiver. Christ was condemned in your place through the very law that you're allowing to continue to condemn you. The lawgiver is the forgiver!

God loves you just as you are, but He loves you too much to leave you as you are. He works on you to make you more like Him. He wants to conform you to His image. For this to happen, you need both humility and gratitude. Humble yourself before God, accept His love and acceptance, and be grateful for what He's done for you.

This is the delicious fruit of holding the two realities in tandem. It is true that you're fallen and in need of grace. But it's also true that God deeply loves you and accepts you in Christ!

When you embrace both of these truths, you won't be eager to go out and do any gross thing that comes into your mind. When you truly understand and appropriate God's grace, you won't *want* to sin anymore. You won't say, "Hey, this afternoon after my haircut, I'm pretty free. I think I'll go do something that I can feel really guilty about."

As you go about your day, tell yourself, "In Christ, I am totally and completely forgiven." Remember that when Christ died on the cross, *all* your sins were still in the future, not just the ones you committed after you came to faith. Christ accepted you knowing exactly who you were, are, and will be. You are totally and completely loved and accepted by God.

When Christ is your Savior, you're on your way to heaven not because you're perfect, but because you are clothed in the perfect righteousness of the One who has imputed His perfection to you. You wear a robe of *His* righteousness. Your best was as filthy rags, and He nailed that to the cross and gave you His spotless clothing so that you now please God.

If you are a Christian and you can't say this, then you are battling against truth and hating what and who God loves. Accept your status as God's beloved and recognize all that He's done for you. Let it become a reality in your life, and tell your wife or kids or friends, "I'm free! I'm free! Thank God I'm free. Jesus Christ set me free. I'm not condemned any longer. I have no right to say about me what He doesn't say about me."

Enjoy your liberty that came in Jesus!

12

Weapon 3: Don't Let Your Sword Get Rusty

After each of our three morning services at Woodstock, I stand in a pastor's reception area to greet visitors. Dozens of people new to the church come through after every service.

One day a guy walked up to me, holding a tape of someone else's sermon. "I've been visiting here for some time, Pastor Hunt," he said. "Do you know this preacher?"

I looked at the tape and said, "No, I don't."

"Well," the man continued, "he claims that Jesus is not God's Son."

By now I'm thinking, *Whoa, time out.*

"Brother," I replied, "let me ask you a question. Have you come to a place in your life where you know for certain you have eternal life?"

"Yes, sir," he said, "I'm saved, I'm saved."

"Okay," I continued, "then let me ask you something else. What have you been studying recently?"

I got a blank stare. "What do you mean, sir?" he asked.

"What portions of God's Word are you studying or putting to

memory? Are you reading any good Christian books that help you grow spiritually?"

"No, sir."

"Have you been through our new members class?"

"No, I just come to worship service."

"My friend," I said, "we can answer every question you have. We can help you to grow if you really want to."

That man had gone into spiritual battle unarmed. What would you think of a soldier, armed with nothing but a smile, who marched into battle against a well-equipped enemy? Would his pearly whites stand much of a chance against a battery of heavy machine guns or a squadron of tanks? Hardly.

In the same way, in our spiritual battle against demonic strongholds, we have to go into the fight fully armed with the divine power of the Word of God, the Bible. Occasionally you'll hear people ask, "How can we make the Bible more relevant to today?" Make it *more relevant*? Are you kidding? It's never irrelevant. It has always been applicable to the needs of people in every generation up through today.

God speaks to us through His Word, challenges us, convicts us, teaches us, encourages us, and corrects us. If you really desire to grow as a believer and become the man you've always wanted to be, then you cannot afford to let your "sword of the Spirit," the Bible, get rusty (see Ephesians 6:17). I hope that by reading this chapter, you will gain a deeper love for the Word of God.

One Little Verse Can Make a Big Difference

Back when I was eighteen years old, I used to visit the Red Fox Saloon several nights a week. I was a pool hustler playing in straight pool tournaments, where we had to call every shot. About the only thing I ever did well was play pool.

But one Sunday I got gloriously saved, and right after that I started going to church every Sunday and Wednesday. Soon there came a day when I said, "I want to give my body to the Lord as a weapon for God." Before that, I had never read a Bible; certainly, I'd never owned one. The day after I got saved, my wife bought me a Bible. Someone told me, "Open it to the book of Matthew and start reading."

You know what first grabbed my heart? The first verse I can remember that profoundly challenged my life was Luke 1:15, a prophecy about John the Baptist: "He will be great in the sight of the Lord, and shall drink neither wine nor strong drink."

I thought, *I've drank enough of that stuff.*

The verse continues, "He will also be filled with the Holy Spirit, even from his mother's womb."

I said, "I want that to be me. I want to be strong for God, not mediocre, not just pussyfooting around." I wanted God to make me into a mighty weapon for His use.

Not long after that, the apostle Paul's words in Romans 6:19-20 spoke to me very personally: "Just as you presented your members as slaves of uncleanness and lawlessness leading to more lawlessness, so now present your members as slaves of righteousness for holiness. For when you were slaves of sin, you were free in regard to righteousness."

I wondered, *What in the world does that mean?* I quickly learned it meant that when I was a slave to sin, before I knew Jesus Christ, I could be at the pool room, have a bottle of beer in one hand and a cigarette in the other, take God's name in vain while trying to win somebody else's money, and then lay down at night and never give any of that a second thought. You know why? I was "free in regard to righteousness."

That's not true of me anymore, thank God. I'm a slave of righteousness. God lives inside of me. You may tell me I did something wrong, but you won't be the first to do so. The Holy Spirit already has spoken through His Word to tell me what I did wrong. You only confirmed what He has already said.

I also learned that when the Bible tells me to reckon myself dead to sin (Romans 6:11), it's speaking very practically. To "reckon" means to count, or consider, or to number something. It refers to having an absolute, unreserved confidence in what your mind knows to be true. I said, "I'm not presenting my life to unrighteousness anymore. You know what I'm going to do? I am going to present myself to God as being alive from the dead. God has said this, and I'm going to take Him at His word."

Such heartfelt confidence directly affects a man's actions and decisions. Paul wasn't referring to some mind game in which we try to trick ourselves into thinking a certain way. Rather, he was urging us to embrace—by faith—what God has revealed in His Word to be true.

Too often we have tried to make the Bible so heavenly sounding that it has lost its pragmatism. But the Bible is pragmatically true; it makes practical sense. My wife recently said to me, "We would not have what we have today if God had not taught us to give what we give." That is a spiritual paradox. How can you give away what you have and still have more? That doesn't make sense. It never will. But it's pragmatically true.

I often wonder, *Where are the men today who want to be strong for God? Where are the men who will take God at His word and act on what they find in His Word?*

Obedience Before Victory

Some people treat the contents of the Bible as mere information, and not as truth to obey. But God's desire is that His Word be obeyed. You read it, and then with the help of the Spirit of God, you bring your life into sync with His truth.

If God would permit me to develop a life message that I could preach to every Christian alive, I'd want to preach a sermon on obedience. *Obedience* is the absolute keyword for the Christian life, not *victory.*

Some men tell me, "I'm praying for victory over such-and-such a stronghold." But you don't have to pray for victory. Pray instead that you will be obedient, because victory is a byproduct of obedience. Victory comes when you obey God. Pray that God will help you to obey.

When God bids you dip in the Jordan River, wash in the Siloam Pool, or walk a desert trail, your victory lies at the end of that process. When God says go, that is not a suggestion, but a command. We have to learn to be sensitive to God and to obey whatever He tells us in His Word.

It's that simple.

When God told Joshua to march around Jericho, obedience had to follow. The marching itself was not the victory, but Joshua's obedience to the divine command to march. Obedience always precedes victory.

Did the residents of Jericho make fun of Joshua? I'm sure they did. "Hey, look, the great general has his men walking around our walls. How stupid! What morons!" I'm sure they cursed Israel. But Joshua let none of that deter him from doing what God had commanded. He instructed his army to march around the city once a day for six days. Then on the seventh day, just as God had commanded, Joshua had the army march around the city seven times, then had the priests blow the trumpets and the people shout. And the walls of the great city crashed to the ground. But Joshua did not get the slightest taste of victory until he first obeyed.

You'll find that same truth applies to your battles against the strongholds in your life. Obedience precedes victory. Always.

A man from another community who had attended one of our men's conferences wrote to me and said, "After the conference, God changed the men of this church. In obedience to God, they began to confess to one another how they were in affairs, and other different sins in their lives. The men got honest before God and went home and told their wives—and that Sunday, we had the greatest and most authentic service of worship before God we've ever known."

Victory is a byproduct of obedience. As we concentrate on living an obedient, holy life, we will surely experience the joy of victory over sin. I believe that if you approach the Bible humbly to obey it, God will speak to your heart about what you need to do.

Nothing breaks the Father's heart more than the disobedience of His children. In 3 John 4, the apostle John wrote, "I have no greater joy than to hear that my children walk in truth."

Oswald Chambers wrote, "If you have received the Spirit and are obeying him, you find he brings your Spirit into complete harmony with God, and the sound of your going and the sound of God's goings are one and the same."[32] E. Stanley Jones said, "If you make a compromise with surrender, you can remain interested in the abundant life, all the riches of freedom, love, and peace, but it is the same as looking at a display in a shop window. You look through the window but do not go in and buy. You will not pay the price—surrender [to Christ]."[33] The great evangelist D.L. Moody said, "Obedience means marching right on whether we feel like it or not."[34]

A Desire for the Word

At one time in my life, I didn't care that I had no Bible. But once I got saved, God put a burning desire in my heart to know and obey His Word. Spiritual growth is always marked by a craving for and a delight in God's Word. First Peter 2:2-3 says, "As newborn babes, desire the pure milk of the word, that you may grow thereby, if indeed you have tasted that the Lord is gracious" (1 Peter 2:2-3).

How does a Christian man nurture a strong desire for the truth of God's Word?

1. By remembering his life's source.

Jesus taught us that we are clean because of the word He has spoken to us (John 15:3). When I got up this morning, I brushed my teeth, shaved, and jumped into the shower. I took a washrag, put soap on it, and cleaned myself on the outside.

Then I went down to my little study, which I consider my prayer room, and I got into the Word. In doing so, God cleaned me up on the inside. This is how you develop a desire for the Word of God—by spending time in it. The Word of God both convicts you and gives you confidence.

2. By eliminating sin from his life.

One day I officiated at a funeral in my hometown of Wilmington, North Carolina. Afterward, my wife and I started walking out of the church to get in our rental car, drive to the airport, and fly home. A couple of ladies who had attended the service were standing around smoking. They recognized me as the pastor who had just performed the funeral service, and with cigarette in hand, one lady said, "Hey, Rev, next time you talk to the man upstairs, ask him to take these cigarettes from me."

Because I was in a hurry, I just chuckled and walked on. But I thought, *First, He's not going to take them. And second, He doesn't want them.*

But wouldn't it be neat if it were that easy? I would like to lose my love handles, for example. It's one of those things that happens to guys my age. I work out for an hour about four days a week, run the treadmill, jog about five miles, but I still have them. Wouldn't it be nice to be able to say, "Lord, I ask in Jesus' name, please take some of this weight off me"?

I believe the Spirit of God would say, "Meet you at the gym."

The Bible instructs me to "lay aside" certain useless things (Hebrews 12:1). Some bad things in my life get eliminated only when I take action, empowered by God's Spirit. God expects me to act in partnership with Him.

Have you tried to eliminate the practical aspect of the Word of God? Imagine someone saying, "I've been praying that the Lord would make me into a morning person." I have my doubts that God would make that happen without any effort on the part of the person making that request. Do you know how I became a morning person? I made a commitment when I started college. I knew I'd be there and in seminary for seven years straight. I took eight o'clock classes, without exception, every semester. Why? So I'd have to get up, do my quiet time, get together with my family, and then go to school. As a result, after years and years of doing this, it has become extremely difficult for me to sleep in. God expects us to act in partnership with Him.

3. By admitting his need for God's truth.

Do you realize how much you need the Word of God? "Your lovingkindness and Your truth will continually preserve me," wrote the psalmist (40:11). The Word guards you, preserves you, keeps you safe. I know it has guarded my life these past forty years.

Many times, the spiritual battle we wage amounts to a war of words, each word contending for your allegiance. The book of Proverbs talks about an immoral woman who will try to seduce you with her words (Proverbs 5:1-10). The only thing you have to successfully combat her words is God's Word. Jesus beautifully exemplified this strategy when the devil tried to tempt Him to do evil. Three times, Jesus quoted the book of Deuteronomy to counter Satan's enticing words (see Matthew 4:1-11).

You and I need the practical warnings in God's Word. For example, Solomon wrote that "The lips of an immoral woman drip honey," comparing them to the sweetest thing he knew, "and her mouth is smoother than oil," comparing them to the smoothest thing in his world (Proverbs 5:3). It may look like honey and it may be smooth as oil, but somebody who's seen it all before assures us, "In the end she is bitter as wormwood, sharp as a two-edged sword" (verse 4). The term "wormwood" speaks of suffering, while the term "sword" refers to death. Solomon had been there. He had fouled up. Today we can learn from his mistakes. God wants to warn us through His Word. And believe me, we need those warnings!

The Word of God will tell you which things you need to get out of your life and which things you need to get in. It will also give you the power to accomplish both. Why do you think Jesus quoted Deuteronomy 8:3 when He said, "Man shall not live by bread alone, but by every word that proceeds from the mouth of God" (Matthew 4:4)? You and I both need the Word.

4. By pursuing spiritual growth.

I'm the chaplain at Dixie Speedway, the fastest-growing 3/8th-mile dirt race track in the United States. From the first week in May through November, unless my wife and I are out of town, I will be there, sharing the gospel of Jesus Christ.

At the track, I give out thousands of the *Jesus* video, thousands of the tape *From the Pool Room to the Pulpit* (my life story), thousands of copies of a short book with an invitation to salvation in Christ at the end. When I set up a table with a hundred books and a hundred tapes, almost all the men will pick up the tape, and almost all the women will pick up the book. For the most part, women are readers, men are not.

While in general many men do not read, we *have* to get back to the Bible, back to the Word of God, back to the book that God wrote, the book that God blesses, the book that has muscle. It describes itself as alive and quick, full of the power of God. The Bible is sharper than any two-edged sword (Hebrews 4:12). No other book is like the Word of God!

I want to *know* that I'm growing in faith. I want to sense the spiritual growth in my life. I want people to see something attractive in my life and then come up to me and say, "What has God been teaching you anyway?"

Answers for *All* of Life's Issues

To succeed in the Christian life, to break down and destroy any strongholds that the enemy might try to build in your life, divine wisdom must have a permanent place in your mind and conduct. You get that divine wisdom in the Word of God.

When I'm talking to an unsaved man on the plane and he finds out I'm a minister, usually he either gets too busy to talk, or he wants to talk. When he wants to talk, it's not unusual for him say, "You have a Bible answer for everything, don't you?" Absolutely, under God!

I haven't found any subject in life that the Bible doesn't speak to. I was on a plane one day and a guy started talking about something related to immorality. "You know," I said, "the righteous man walks in his integrity; his children are blessed after him."[35]

"Hey, say that *slower*," the man said. So I did.

"Who said that?" he asked.

"Solomon," I answered.

"Don't think I've read him. Where'd you get his book?"

Know your Bible!

Occasionally I write articles for the local newspaper. Sometimes instead of signing my name, I'll sign the name of the Bible author I've quoted. For example, if I've quoted a great statement from 2 Corinthians, I'll sign it "Paul." If I were to cite 2 Corinthians as the source, people would complain. Instead, they read it and enjoy it and the quotation sparks all kinds of community buzz. I've even heard people talking in a restaurant: "Did you see that article in the paper today?"

"Yeah!"

Most people in our culture have not heard that the Bible contains great and wonderful truth. But in fact, it is overflowing with life-giving truth. Are you taking advantage of it?

Pray the Word

The Bible reminds us that every believer has two primary weapons to use against the enemy's strongholds: God's Word and prayer. Paul tells us that we have "the sword of the Spirit, which is the word of God," and then he reminds us to be "praying always" (Ephesians 6:17-18).

May I suggest that you learn to pray the Word of God? In her book *Praying God's Word*, Beth Moore has written, "Strongholds cannot be swept away with a spiritual broom. We can't fuss at them or make them flee. We can't ignore them until they disappear. Strongholds are broken one way only: *they have to be demolished.*"[36]

Have you ever seen the demolition of a high-rise building? Workers strategically place dynamite in various parts of the building, and then initiate a controlled detonation. You can do a similar thing in the spiritual realm. Take the two primary sticks of dynamite God has given you—prayer and the Word—strap them together, ignite them with faith, and then watch what God will do. Let me give you a couple of simple examples of how you can practically marry God's Word and prayer.

You might start by reading Proverbs 3:33, which declares, "The curse of the LORD is on the house of the wicked, but He blesses the home of the just." Take that good word, and then personalize it in prayer: "Lord God, Your Word says You bless the home of the righteous, and that Your curse is on the home of the wicked. Lord, please help me cleanse my home of any kind of material that supports or fuels wickedness. Make this the kind of home that You can fully bless."

Then there is Proverbs 4:23-24, which says, "Keep your heart with all diligence, for out of it spring the issues of life. Put away from you a deceitful mouth, and put perverse lips far from you." To be perverse or deceitful means to wander off the path. God wants us on the straight and narrow, but sometimes we drift away from it. So I pray, "Lord God, help me to guard my heart above all else, for it's the wellspring of my life. Help me to put away perversity from my mouth and keep corrupt talk far from my lips." It really is that simple, but it packs an amazing punch.

As I've mentioned, I have a room in my home where, every morning, I spend a minimum of forty-five minutes with the Lord. There I get my mind focused so I can hear from God and get His battle plan for the day. Why? I desire to finish well. I want to make a positive mark in this life. I want to influence people's lives for God and for good. Don't you?

Counterattack!

I believe we men can change a great deal in our culture if we'll just learn to be godly. A devotional life is so indispensable to this pursuit that I can't imagine succeeding without it.

When you're a devotional Christian who wants to think right, you read the Word of God when you first get up. It becomes like a searchlight from heaven, showing the inner recesses and dark crevasses of your mind. Someone put it this way: "Every man is like the moon. They all have a dark side." The Word of God allows the light of God's revelation to shine into your life so it can bring about change.

I'm in a discipleship group with five men. Most weeks we memorize together four to five verses of Scripture. It's amazing what happens when you lock Scripture in your brain! When you saturate your mind with the Word of God, you have what you need to win the battle. When the enemy pounds you with his artillery, you'll be able to counterattack at a moment's notice with God's Word.

Pulling down strongholds is no easy task! So whenever you find yourself in the heat of battle, remember this: The greatest power in the whole world is the Holy Spirit, moving in lockstep with the Word of God.

Bank on it and win.

13

Weapon 4: Practice Walking in the Spirit

At a restaurant one day, I was getting ready to give thanks for a meal. My wife and I asked the waitress, "Can we pray for you about anything?"

Immediately the young woman started to cry. "My daddy died a year ago today. He was my best friend. I am really struggling. Thank you for asking. Will you pray for me? I probably need to be here and be busy at work, instead of just sitting at home and thinking about my daddy all day long."

She wept and continued to bring me coffee after coffee. "I just have to ask," she said at one point, "I can't believe that you asked to pray for me on the day that is the most difficult day of my life. Nobody has ever done this. Are you an angel?"

My wife just sat there, rolling her eyes. I pointed to the love of my life and said to the waitress, "Ask her."

"He's no angel," Janet declared. "He has no wings. Some days, he has a pitchfork."

None of us on this earth ever reaches a level of perfection. Sin will knock at the front door, and if you won't let it in, it will run around to the back door. If you don't let it in there, it'll try crawling in your windows. It doesn't care which way you let it in; it just wants in.

While the message of Galatians 2:20 is gloriously true, our experience of it varies. Paul wrote, "I have been crucified with Christ; it is no longer I who live, but Christ lives in me; and the life which I now live in the flesh I live by faith in the Son of God, who loved me and gave Himself for me." I love those days when my experience is "Not I, but Christ." But I have to confess, there are other days when it's "Not Christ, but I."

Why is that? And how can we get to the point where it's more the first experience than the second?

An Internal War

A war is going on in all of us. "The flesh lusts against the Spirit and the Spirit against the flesh" (Galatians 5:17). Two contrary things are going on in our lives, and because of this, "you do not do the things that you wish."

I want to be a Spirit-controlled Christian. I want to influence others for Jesus. I want, most of all, to glorify God. I want to make much of Him. I want to make the name of Jesus famous. But I can't do any of that unless I let the Spirit fill me and lead me. Adrian Rogers used to say, "The only way you'll succeed in the Christian life is to be filled with the Holy Spirit—and then you'll struggle."

While the cross renders sin inoperative, that doesn't mean sin is dead. It can still exert itself. The Bible says we are dead to sin (Romans 6:11), but it doesn't say that sin died. Sin is still very much alive. It constantly hounds us.

Nowhere does the Bible mean to imply that the crucifixion analogy carries the idea of total death, in which all sinful influence ceases. Not until someone literally dies do *all* influences cease. A dead body does neither good nor evil. It's dead.

But Paul called sin a reality in his life (and in mine and yours). The temptations of the world are still very real. When I came to

Christ, the unredeemed self really was crucified and I really was born a new person in Jesus. I am now dead toward the world—but the world is not dead. It's still out there, trying to draw me in.

Because of my relationship with Jesus Christ, however, I am free to serve Jesus, and I can achieve a lot of victory. In one sense, the power of the old self and of the world have been broken. These influences, even though they still exist, no longer *have* to dominate me. Sin still resides in me, but it doesn't have to reign in me. And it doesn't have to reign in you either.

A Sinner Saved by Grace

As Christians, we are sinners saved by grace. Some people get upset at this idea and say, "No, we are the righteousness of God in Christ." Absolutely.

"We are also filled with the Spirit," they say. Yes, that is true as well.

They go on: "He's imparted all this to you, and you have everything you need for life." Yes—but we are still sinners.

Even as believers, sin still dwells in us—that is, in our body. And the Spirit of God dwells in us too. They're contrary to one another, and they battle one another. I've been a Christian for more than forty years, and I know there's no seniority in the Christian life. You never get to the point where you can say, "Thank God that's behind me." No, sin is always right there, beside you or in front of you, babbling. Sometimes I tell people, "I feel as though the battle has intensified."

Many years ago a pastor wrote to me, "I am having a real struggle as a pastor. How long were you at your church before you quit having this type of problem?"

I wrote him back and said, "I will notify you when it happens." I've not written that note yet.

Someone once told me, "Don't tell the people in your church they are sinners, or they'll act like it." They're going to act like it anyway. I don't want everyone trying to conceal their sin from themselves and the fellowship. If we do that, we'll all remain alone with our sin, living in lust and hypocrisy.

You may feel as though you're the only one who struggles, but you're not. Dietrich Bonhoeffer said, "He who is alone with his sin is utterly alone...The pious fellowship permits no one to be a sinner."[37] The fact is, we *are* sinners. I'm right there with Dietrich Bonhoeffer.

I know I've been saved. I know that the Spirit of God dwells in me and that I am different from what I was before. But I still have struggles. I still have battles. I don't always win. The good news is that the enemy doesn't win nearly as much as he used to.

We fall down, and God helps us up. I wish I could say I've never stumbled, that I have no regrets, that I've never spoken any words I wish I could retrieve or done anything I wish I could take back. But I can't.

Do you know what I really want? I want God to help me to feel *before* I sin the way I feel *after* I've sinned. When I respond in a sinful way to something, the Spirit of God within me says, "Johnny, you didn't react right." That's what made me call my wife last night to say, "I want you to forgive me for saying something negative about so-and-so."

So how do sinful people like us move forward?

First, each of us must receive Jesus Christ as Lord and Savior. Christ died on the cross to make a way for the whole world to be forgiven, but it is up to individuals to repent of their sin and embrace and receive God's forgiveness and cleansing in the person of Jesus Christ.

"Okay, *now* it's over!" someone says. "Thank God, that's done."

No, it's just the beginning

"But that doesn't make sense," someone says. "I became a Christian this week and you wouldn't believe all the hell that broke loose."

Actually, I do believe it. Before a person becomes saved, he is walking the same way that the people of the world walk, the same way the devil himself walks. But when he repents, does an about-face, and gets saved, he's walking with the Lord. Instead of walking with the devil, he's walking against him. This helps to explain why the Christian life can feel so exhausting at times. It's the reason so many men say, "I can't do it. It's too difficult."

No, the Christian life is not difficult. The Christian life is impossible. Only Christ can live it. The only hope you have is Jesus, who overcomes for you and lives His life through you. It's Christ in you, the hope of glory (see Colossians 1:27). You need to give Jesus control of your life. Only then will you experience victory.

Imagine you're driving down the road and you unintentionally cut someone off. He pulls up beside you and flips the middle finger of fellowship at you. Humanly, you want to respond the same way. But instead, you say, "I'm so sorry. I didn't even see you back there."

Where did that come from? It's Christ in you.

Wouldn't you like to stop responding from the sinful flesh and instead, have Christ's response come from within you?

Do you want to respond in a godly way when the challenge comes? How is that possible? When you don't walk according to the flesh but according to the Spirit. You don't have to walk in your own energy. You can walk in the power of God, the Holy Spirit.

A New Way to Walk

The Bible instructs us, "Walk in the Spirit, and you shall not fulfill the lust of the flesh" (Galatians 5:16). The term translated "walk" speaks of a progression. It's not that I've walked far enough and now everything is behind me. "Walk" is in the present tense, which means I still have a journey in front of me. Much of that journey is filled with struggles.

The word "walk" also implies control. When God tells us to walk in the Spirit, it means we must be willingly controlled by the Spirit. To walk in the Spirit, be led by the Spirit, or live in the Spirit means to yield—all three refer to the same thing.

And why should we walk in the Spirit? So we will not fulfill the lust of the flesh. Even though the Lord Jesus has come to reign in our life, we can still let the flesh have its way.

The Spirit directs a godly man's earthly conduct. The Bible says that when you walk in the Spirit—when you depend on God's power to enable you to act in a godly way even when no one is looking and even in the areas where you believe it's impossible for you to get caught—you will not fulfill the lusts of the flesh. Walking in the Spirit is an imperative. God does not make this merely optional. Walking in the Spirit is patterned after the teaching and example of Jesus (see Matthew 4:1; Luke 4:1,14).

When you obey, you find yourself loving in the face of hatred and experiencing peace in the midst of chaos and grief. When you move beyond God's boundaries and the Spirit speaks to you, you make course adjustments. If He convicts you and you're not willing to make the course adjustments, you backslide. When you make the course adjustments, you start growing again. You fall down, but you get up: "A righteous man may fall seven times and rise again" (Proverbs 24:16).

The Spirit of God depresses your evil cravings. This doesn't come from you, because something in you sees the evil as appetizing. The old you is still there, battling. But if the Spirit of God is controlling you, He enables you to respond correctly to those evil cravings.

It is the Holy Spirit that convicts you of wrong activities or attitudes and causes you to say, "I've been doing something that displeases Jesus. I surrender. I confess to God. I repent." You may even confess, "This is going to be a struggle in my life, but going forward, I want Jesus to rule in me. I don't want to be dominated by that fleshly craving anymore." The Spirit of God then depresses that craving in you.

Note that the apostle Paul said, "Walk in the Spirit, and you *shall not* fulfill the lust of the flesh" (Galatians 5:16). That's an ironclad promise. The active presence of Christ in your life makes it possible for you to completely set aside the lust of the flesh. Only by the Spirit of God can you properly handle your sinful, fleshly desires.

Do you want to live your life in submission to Jesus Christ, or do you want a self-centered, self-serving, self-absorbed life of sin? Jesus can empower you to love what God loves and to hate what God hates. But you have to make the choice, every day and every moment of every day, to walk in the Spirit.

A Choice to Make

We can either produce the works of the flesh or the fruit of the Spirit. When our lives produce the works of the flesh, it's because we are not choosing to allow the Spirit of God to control us. We don't need to go to a human counselor and say, "What do you think about this? Is this right or wrong?" The Spirit of God, our divine counselor, has already made that clear to us.

I don't want to fulfill the lust of the flesh, and I doubt that you want to. I want to walk in the Spirit. So I must choose to be a Spirit-controlled, Spirit-filled believer.

Scripture presents to us a list of the ugly characteristics of spiritual failure right next to a list of the beautiful traits of spiritual success. Study for a bit the following products of a life lived in the flesh, contrasted with a life lived in the Spirit (see Galatians 5:19-23):

List One		List Two
adultery	outbursts of wrath	love
fornication	selfish ambitions	joy
uncleanness	dissensions	peace
lewdness	heresy	longsuffering
idolatry	envy	kindness
sorcery	murders	goodness
hatred	drunkenness	faithfulness
contentions	revelries	gentleness
jealousies		self-control

If you choose to let your flesh have its way, the characteristics in the first list will dominate your life. You may try to be a good guy, but you won't be a godly guy.

Take a good, long look at your own life. Be brutally frank. Would you say you have more in common with the first list, or the second? If you are showing more of the traits in the first list than the second, cry out to God and say, "Lord, help me. I want to live out the traits in the second list."

Understand, though, that list two can characterize your life only as you choose to yield to the Spirit. Confess your sins to God and, by faith, say, "Lord, fill me with the Holy Spirit. Help me to walk in the Spirit." And how do you do that? Colossians 2:6 says, "As you therefore have received Christ Jesus the Lord, so walk in Him." How did you receive Jesus into your life at the time of salvation? By faith. So how do you walk in Him? By faith. You take Him at His Word.

The Miracle of Transformation

The miracle of the Christ life is one of transformation: "We all, with unveiled face, beholding as in a mirror the glory of the Lord, are being transformed into His image from glory to glory, just as by the Spirit of the Lord" (2 Corinthians 3:18). The Spirit of God wants to work in your life to transform you from the inside out.

A while back, God put this verse so powerfully on my heart that I meditated on it for a whole year. Every morning for 365 days, I'd ponder it. And I'd pray, "God, teach me this verse. Teach me this verse!" I became so intrigued and moved by its message that I wrote seven sermons based on it. God used that verse powerfully in the life and growth of our church.

While I am not yet all that I want to be, I have progressed over the past forty years. I am not what I used to be. God, through His Spirit, is growing me more into the likeness of Jesus. I pray that the older I get, the more I'll continue to grow.

As we're faithful to imitate Christ and follow lovingly in His steps, the Holy Spirit does something through us that we could never do by mere imitation. He manifests in our lives the actual life of Christ. Of course, no one can ever become like Christ *only* by imitation. A transformation has to take place in which Christ changes a man from the inside out. It's not the imitation of Christ that makes the key difference, but a transformation by Christ.

You and I need Jesus Christ to change us. And here's what is key: We have to *want* Him to change us. When we become desperate for Christ to change us, then a transformation is able to take place.

Are you desperate for that transformation?

Transformation is God's response to your crying out for help from a deep sense of inadequacy and humility, and your striving by the Spirit to imitate Christ as you bear spiritual fruit. You humble yourself before God and cry out, "I cannot live this life! It's Christ in me that is the hope of glory. It's Jesus living this life through me."

Many theologians call this "the exchanged life." You have to give Jesus your life, because you cannot accomplish this transformation on your own. And then He gives you His life in exchange. If there's anything beautiful in you that brings glory to God, it's Christ in you and the transformation that He's bringing about in you.

The Bible says, very clearly, "If anyone is in Christ, he is a new creation" (2 Corinthians 5:17). That is a profound statement, and it's a matter of fact, not mere wishful thinking. You *are* a new creation. You are *not* the person you were. You've been recreated, born again. Old things have passed away. All things have become new. Every day, in fact, God wants to show you new things. As you behold Christ, God transforms you into the image of Christ. When you wake up in the morning and start thinking about the Lord Jesus and open His Word, you open the door for transformation.

The Bible says the life of Jesus is being manifested in your mortal flesh (2 Corinthians 4:11). But how does that happen? It happens through your dying and Christ living through you.

Now, transformation is not constant! In fact, it's proportional to your beholding, which is often intermittent. If you're not careful in your walk with the Spirit, you may find yourself stumbling: "Let him who thinks he stands take heed lest he fall" (1 Corinthians 10:12). We all have to *deliberately* abide in Christ. Adrian Rogers put it this way: "Since I've been saved, I sin all I want to. And I don't want to sin anymore."

Stop Stirring the Dust

When I was in college, I had to read John Bunyan's *Pilgrim's Progress* in older-style English. That's not easy for someone who struggles with today's English! But the story so intrigued me that I found a simplified version and quickly and deeply fell in love with the book.

John Bunyan, an English minister in the 1600s, was thrown into jail for preaching the gospel. While there, he wrote this allegory about the Christian life. He told a story about Pilgrim, a young man who was journeying through life and hoping to end up in the Celestial City. The allegory teaches many things related to the Christian life. An assortment of characters comes into Pilgrim's life, teaching him crucial lessons through a variety of events that occur in different places.

In one of my favorite scenes, Bunyan describes how Pilgrim visits Interpreter's house. Since the house is completely covered in dust, Pilgrim takes a broom and starts to sweep. He soon begins to choke from the great cloud of dust that he stirs up. The more vigorously he sweeps, the more suffocating the dust becomes. Interpreter then orders a maid to sprinkle the room with water, which completely washes away the dust.

Interpreter explains to Pilgrim that the house represents the heart of an unsaved man, covered in the dust of original sin. The man with the broom symbolizes the law, trying to do good and be good, working vigorously, and yet getting further and further behind. The maid with the water is the gospel. The point of the story is that all the law can do is stir up sin, but the gospel of Jesus Christ can wash it away.

Are you tired of stirring the dust? It's suffocating. Maybe you've been trying to be good enough to live the Christian life and yet all your efforts have led to nothing but frustration. At the end of the day, it seems like you're further behind than you were when you started. You think, *I am defeated, defeated, defeated. Is there any hope for me?*

Yes, there's hope! But you must remember that the Spirit of God leads contrary to the flesh. Your flesh wants its appetites satisfied. If you've been careless, allowing your eyes to go places your flesh wants them to go, the devil shoots an arrow that hits its mark. He wastes no arrows; he won't shoot at a heart surrounded by the armor of God.

You are in trouble if you choose not to appropriate what God has provided to enable you to stand. It's not that you don't have the right armor; it's just that you've been unwilling to wear it. You've chosen not to appropriate it.

Every believing man still has sin within him that has not been totally eradicated. A battle continues to rage—and Jesus desires to deliver you from the power of sin. He doesn't want sin to dominate your life anymore. He wants you to be dominated by His Holy Spirit so that your life takes on the evidence of Him living and ruling in you.

Moving Toward Victory

I have an intense craving, a deep desire, even a passion to live a Spirit-controlled life. I really want others to see Christ in me and so be encouraged, instead of observing a defeated Christian who cannot bring glory to God.

I want the power of the Holy Spirit to so control me that I can say no to sin more often. I am grateful that God lifts me up when I fall down, but I want to be so filled with His Spirit that I will make the right decision to start with. I want to walk more consistently in victory.

I expect you want the same thing. You wouldn't have read this far if you didn't! But I can also imagine that you may feel distraught at the fierceness of the battle.

Be encouraged that God already has done everything you need for victory. Yes, it's a struggle, but it's a struggle you can win. Start to imagine right now the difference that God can make in this world through your choice to live a Spirit-filled life.

Oswald Chambers wrote, "If you have received the Spirit and are obeying Him, you find He brings your spirit into complete harmony with God."[38] That's powerful encouragement! And the best part is that you can know, even today, that you are moving in the same direction as the Spirit.

14

Weapon 5: Lean on Your Brothers in Arms

I'll never forget it for as long as I live.

A lot of people say that "Tim" (name changed) looks like me, although I'm older than he is. We're about the same size. We're still close friends. We used to be in the same vocation—but no longer.

Tim had a lovely wife and pastored a good church. At some point, however, he started contemplating a very different path. His wife sensed trouble ahead and warned him about it, but Tim assured her, "No sirree, that's not a problem here."

In all my years of ministry, I can't recall dealing with any person who, before things really went south, failed to get a warning from *someone*. This would have been a great time for Tim to say, "It's amazing the perception that God has given you, honey, because I am struggling. Thanks. You've thrown me a lifeline." But he didn't say it, and his life continued to barrel down the same deadly path.

His wife told me later that she'd thought about calling me to voice her concerns, but she didn't want to embarrass her mate. Plus, she wondered, what would Tim do if he found out she'd called? She didn't want to lose her husband. Would he leave her, saying, "If you can't trust me, then we might as well not be together"?

I was supposed to be Tim's role model. On more than one occasion, he had named me as the guy he had chosen as his mentor. But I didn't find out about any of what had happened until it was too late.

One day Tim and his wife drove several hours to sit with me in a restaurant. I'll never forget what he said to me. "This is the hardest meeting," he began. That's never a great sign. "I've already told my daddy what I'm getting ready to tell you," he continued, "but I'm finding it harder to tell you than it was to tell him."

Wow, I thought. What was coming next could not be good.

In a halting voice filled with great shame, Tim described how he had gotten sexually involved with his secretary. The pair had gotten involved in an adulterous relationship, and as soon as the church found out, Tim was shown the door.

"I can remember where I was sitting when I first contemplated all of this," Tim confessed. "I felt like I was drowning."

Not long afterward, Tim found himself on his way to the Southern Baptist Convention. "I wanted to meet with you there, Pastor Johnny," he remembered, "either early one morning or one night after the conference. I was going to ask if you and I could go to some quiet place where I could tell you, 'I'm struggling with something and I need your help.' I rehearsed it all in my mind."

I can still picture the scene in the restaurant. As Tim spoke, his words seemed to tumble out almost in slow motion.

"I felt that you would have thrown me a lifeline with a preserver and pulled me in," Tim continued. "You would have helped me, because that's what friends do."

But my friend never got around to asking for help, or asking for the meeting. Instead, he let the divinely appointed lifeline slip out of his hands. Why?

"Even though I had not done anything wrong yet," he explained, "embarrassment stopped me. I just kept thinking, *I can handle it. I've got it. It's just a propensity to sin. I don't have to give in to it."*

Tim knew all the relevant Bible verses. He'd preached on many of them and could quote several by heart, including this one: "Though we walk in the flesh, we do not war according to the flesh. For the weapons of our warfare are not carnal but mighty in God for pulling down strongholds, casting down arguments and every high thing that exalts itself against the knowledge of God, bringing every thought into captivity to the obedience of Christ" (2 Corinthians 10:3-5).

He thought he could handle the situation on his own.

He was wrong.

Tim didn't fall because he was weak. Proverbs 7:26 makes it clear that *strong* men fall to sexual sin: "She [the adulteress] has cast down many wounded, and all who were slain by her were strong men." If you look in the Bible, you'll find that yes, even the strong can fall into sexual sin. Remember David, the man after God's own heart? And what about Solomon? There was no one wiser.

In His great grace, God gave warnings and gave opportunities to escape, but these men didn't grab the lifelines thrown to them. They didn't listen to God. And in the end, their illicit liaisons led them to ruin.

In this final chapter, I want to say as strongly as I know how that *it takes an army to demolish a stronghold.* You can't whip the devil and his minions on your own. None of us can. That's why God so often instructs us in His Word to engage the enemy with our brothers at our sides.

All of us need the help of other men. We need each other's counsel, encouragement, warnings, and mutual accountability. If you try to win alone, you will instead lose alone—and the whole world will see your collapse.

A Common, Deadly Error

Several years ago I played in a golf tournament where I had the opportunity to spend some time with Steve Farrar, author of a number of excellent men's books, including *Finishing Strong*. Steve loves to challenge Christian men to get serious about their personal daily walk with God.

I loved our conversation that day for several reasons, including the surprising fact that someone had introduced Steve to some of my own men's materials, and he wanted to discuss what he had read. But the thing that made the strongest impression on me during our time together was a comment he made about the work of one of his former professors, the late Howard Hendricks, who taught for decades at Dallas Theological Seminary.

Steve told me about a study that "Prof" had done regarding 246 ministers of the gospel who had all fallen morally over a period of two years. All of them had lost their ministries, and many had lost their families. Dr. Hendricks did something bold—he contacted each of the 246 ministers, even if he didn't know them, and asked if he could interview them. They all agreed, and he conducted his interviews either in written form or over the phone. He then compiled and analyzed the responses he had collected.

While Dr. Hendricks noted a host of issues in these men's lives, he identified four characteristics in particular that all (or nearly all) 246 had in common. As Steve described the study, I immediately reached for my pen. I didn't want to miss anything.

The one characteristic identified by Dr. Hendricks that especially took away my breath was the first one he had listed: None of these men were involved in a personal accountability group. Either they didn't see the need, or they thought they were beyond it. It's a scary day when a supposed man of God says, "I don't need to be accountable to anyone about how I live. I'm accountable to the Lord alone."

The other three characteristics all stemmed off of the first one. Dr. Hendricks noted that:

- Each of the men had essentially abandoned a time of daily prayer, Bible reading, and worship.

- More than 80 percent of the men had become sexually involved with the "other woman" after spending significant time with her, often in counseling settings.

- Each of the 246 former ministers had felt certain that this sort of fall "would never happen to me."

Every now and then someone asks me, "Pastor, how do men make it when they don't live their lives devotionally?" While that's a good question, I think I have a better one:

Who said they *are* making it?

The book of Ecclesiastes tells us that it's easy for one to become overpowered (4:12). It's good to have someone who can help you. In fact, it's imperative.

Do you have someone like that?

Who Can You Call?

We all need spiritually mature brothers in our lives. I believe every man ought to have a Paul in his life to help mature him, a Barnabas to help encourage him, and a Timothy into whom he is pouring his life. We all need a mentor, an encourager, and an apprentice. *Every* man ought to have these three relationships in his life. I can name the men in my life who fit all three categories. In His grace, God has put them there.

I've been under mutual, personal accountability for many years with four or five men. These mature, trustworthy friends hold me accountable to be the man God wants me to be. The older I get, the more these friends mean to me. In some special ways, a number of men in my church mean more to me than any family members. Some of them mean things to me that my dad never meant to me. We share a bond, a brotherhood, a friendship.

If you've never had this blessing in your life, I can tell you what will happen the instant you try to initiate such relationships. As soon as you get honest with yourself and say, "I'm coming clean before God and I'm going to find a mature brother in Christ to help me," Satan will say to you, "You know, don't you, that the moment you tell others what you're struggling with, they will write you off? They'll despise you. You would be a lot smarter to just keep quiet."

That's a lie. They won't write you off; they'll admire you.

Find a mature brother in the Lord and ask him to become your accountability partner. Find *someone*. Talk to your pastor. Get in touch with a church staff member. Find a peer, your Sunday school teacher, *someone* you consider to be a godly man, and share with him your struggles.

Find someone who, when you're in trouble, you know you can call him. You can ask him to pray for you, to help you. You don't want to call just anybody; you want a man or men who know how to get hold of God.

On one occasion I brought to church an 88-year-old converted Jewish woman to pray for anyone who needed special deliverance. That woman knew how to get a hold of God! It was almost scary—in a good way—when she started praying. Who do you have like that?

Are You Getting Healed?

You may still doubt whether you *really* need personal accountability in your life. If so, you'll want to read Proverbs 28:13: "He who covers his sins will not prosper, but whoever confesses and forsakes them will have mercy."

You might hear that and reply, "Listen, the Lord Jesus is my accountability partner. I confess my sin to Him. Nobody else needs to know about it."

While that may sound spiritual, may I ask you a question? Do you ever find yourself in a cycle of confessing the same sin over and over again, year in and year out, and yet you never get beyond confessing it? Why is that? Why have you been unable to forsake it? I believe I know the answer, but I doubt you'll like it. Based on my observations, I can say categorically that no man is genuinely sincere about forsaking some persistent sin in his life unless he is willing not only to confess it to the Lord, but also to a mature Christian brother.

"Now hold on," you may say. "Where do you get that?"

Let me direct you to my favorite book in the Bible, James, where you'll find this amazing promise: "Confess your trespasses to one another, and pray for one another, that you may be healed. The effective, fervent prayer of a righteous man avails much" (James 5:16). A lot of men are confessing their sin to God, but they're not getting healed of it. Why not?

The answer is that although they're telling God about their problem, they're staying in the problem. They commit the sin and confess it, then recommit it and reconfess it, then recommit it and reconfess it, over and over and over again. They'll *never* forsake it—and truly find God's mercy—until they find one or more godly, faithful men and say to them, "Guys, I need your help. I'm trapped. This has become a stronghold in my life, and I want God to set me free."

I am told that more than one leading Christian psychologist claims that in the average evangelical church on any given Sunday morning, at least a quarter of the men in attendance are addicted to Internet pornography. Do you think most of them are confessing their sin to God? Probably. Do you think most of them are confessing their sin to a mature Christian brother? Probably not. And so they stay in bondage. They remain prisoners of a stronghold.

What I see going on today amazes me. I'm told that for every man who's hooked on Internet pornography, there's a woman in a chat room. Three pastor friends of mine fell morally within a three-month period. All three of them found a girlfriend in a chat room. None of them told anyone about their struggle until their lives imploded.

To break the power of sin in your life, you need to get the sin out of the shadows, where it grows big and strong, and into the light. You need to tell a mature Christian man about your struggles. That's a significant way to break sin's power over you—and as we've just seen, that's not my idea, but God's.

Many guys have told me, "I felt so grieved after I did it. I confessed it to God. I'd get up the next morning and still have my quiet time. I'd continue to faithfully give at church, maybe even help in other ways. But I couldn't get free until I cared enough to bring a mature brother in and say to him, 'I need you to hold me accountable. I need you to know about this struggle in my life.'"

Tell Your Wife

A woman and her husband came down to see me one day. They came because the woman's husband chose to tell her about some of his hidden struggles. She so appreciated his honesty! Most women love such honesty.

"Pastor," she told me, "God is working in our lives together. My husband never would have shared with me about his struggles with pornography unless God had already been at work in him. He's trying to help me to understand what he's facing—but I want you to know that there are issues in my life too."

Remember, if we cover our sins, we will not prosper. You just can't get ahead if you keep covering up your sin. But the man who confesses his sin and forsakes it will find mercy. So long as we keep our sin private, we'll never gain the power to forsake it. Sin grows strong in the shadows, but wilts in the light.

Let me encourage you to tell your wife about your struggles. Commit both your soul and your struggles to her. Remember, the Bible says the truth will set you free (John 8:32), and your wife needs to hear the truth. Oh, I know what Satan says. "That's a lie!" he shrieks. "The truth will get you rejected. It'll get you ridiculed, embarrassed, sidelined. Is that what you want?"

Ignore him. Cover your ears. Listen to Jesus. And tell your wife the truth. She deserves to know.

The City of Refuge

God put a desire in my heart several years ago to open what we call the City of Refuge. We designed it to help pastors and ministers recover from some sort of spiritual or vocational fall, often caused by personal misconduct.

Because I've been a pastor for a long time, I know that pastors tend to spend a lot of their time dealing with the personal problems of others. Most of my office appointments involve individuals going through some kind of private struggle. It's not unusual for a man to tell me, "I'm in an affair," or "My wife is having an affair," or "My children are strung out on drugs." Here's the bottom line: As a pastor, I spend a large amount of my time in the office dealing with men and their sin. It takes a lot of encouragement to deal regularly with all that!

But what happens when that same pastor—the one who helps his church family deal with their sins—finds his own life touched by some sin, whether in his life or in that of his family? Unfortunately, there's a very good chance that the very same people who asked him for help will tell him to leave. I have never quite understood that dynamic, but it happens all the time. God broke my heart when I saw this occur over and over again.

So one day I said, "I'm going to open a refuge. When a man falls—whether it involves a moral failure, or some financial impropriety, or he's burned out, or even if he's done a good job and his former church just didn't want to change so it could grow—if he calls us for help, we're going to find him somewhere to live. We're going to take care of him until he gets healthy again." If at all possible, we want to keep these men involved in ministry in some way.

As a result, we've helped many ministers and their families. God is helping us, and it's a great joy for me and our church to see how

God can use us to encourage these men and help them and love on them and let them know that there are people out there who still care.

Hard to Keep Warm Alone

Men need other men in their lives. Ecclesiastes 4:11 implies it's a bad deal when a man gets cold and has no one to help him keep warm. That verse, in fact, played a part in prompting our church to begin a street ministry.

Our team preaches and ministers to anywhere from 300 to 800 street people every Thursday night in Atlanta. Rain, sleet, or snow, it doesn't matter. The street people look for our team to arrive. The members of our team preach the gospel, feed the people, and hand out coats and blankets. We call it Church on the Street.

Some of the men we minister to have told us that the only way they can keep from freezing to death in winter is to huddle together. They survive by taking advantage of the body heat of others. These men know they need others to help them stay warm when it gets very cold.

I'm grateful for all the men in my life who keep me warm when I grow a little cold spiritually. God wants to use all of us to help and encourage each other. Life can get cold! It's not just about going to church and looking for what we can get out of it. What if God wants you in a specific congregation because He knows you and your history or background could be a great source of encouragement to another man? What if you're the one man in a thousand miles who could bring desperately needed help to another man in trouble...but you choose not to show up because you say, "Sorry, but this church just doesn't meet my needs"?

Men need other men in their lives, not only to hold each other accountable, but to give each other encouragement and hope. When doctors diagnosed me not long ago with prostate cancer, I found it hard to tell others. And I didn't find it a lot easier once I'd successfully undergone treatment. I didn't like talking about it.

But as a follower of Jesus, you want to help others. When people know you've made it through a dark time in your life, they want to know how you managed it. If they see you once again experiencing joy unspeakable, they want to know how you did it. "Hey, tell me how I can go forward too!" So in my case, I've chosen to tell my story more freely than I would normally.

I learned some of this from David, after the king had sinned terribly. His wicked actions had dearly cost both him and his family. But David didn't crawl into a hole. He didn't retreat from life or allow himself to get bitter. He didn't keep silent about the whole sordid episode. Instead, he said, "I'm not wasting my sorrows. I'm not throwing this away. I'm going to invest this into generations to come. I believe the Holy Spirit is going to let me help those who will come after me. I want to show them how to move forward."

Have you made it through some difficult struggles in life? Are you overcoming some hurtful troubles right now? If so, are there other men in your circles who need to hear about it. How do you think God might want to use your story to help and encourage other men?

Disciplines of a Godly Man

While the last thing I care about is trying to sell you a book, I do want to briefly note one that I mentioned earlier. Over the past decade, I've read about fifty books a year addressed to men. The best one, in my opinion, is *The Disciplines of a Godly Man* by Kent Hughes.

I've not only read it, I've studied it with my accountability group. We discussed one chapter each week. The book has thirty chapters, and each chapter is about ten pages long. We would sit down together and discuss the principles that Hughes developed. Then we'd commit to holding each other accountable to flesh out in our lives every one of the disciplines we discussed.

Do you have someone in your life who's growing with you in the Lord? If you don't, find someone. Don't put it off. Then identify a good day of the week and name a time (early in the morning, breakfast, lunch, whatever) that works for both of you to meet for forty-five minutes to an hour. Set aside that time for the two of you to study together both the Word of God and a good Christian book, such as *The Disciplines of a Godly Man*. Pray for one another and hold each other accountable to *be* godly men. Lord knows we need more of them!

Break Free of the Cycle

As we've seen throughout this book, most Christian men are on a wearisome cycle of obedience/disobedience to God. At some point—maybe after a major personal indiscretion, maybe after a great Sunday morning church service, maybe at a men's conference, or maybe after getting scared out of their wits by something devastating that happens to a friend or acquaintance—they'll reach a critical moment and ask God to forgive them and cleanse them. They realize that they need to make some hard commitments, and they do.

But before long, they're back where they started, feeling guilty and miserable all over again. And the old, agonizing cycle repeats once more.

Have you ever *really* wanted to break the cycle? Seriously, under God, wouldn't you like to be free?

Sin is too big to be handled alone. When you make yourself mutually accountable to other Christian brothers, you're all saying to one another, "I'm talking to my Father about this temptation on your behalf." If you want to break the strongholds that keep you bound, you really don't have any other choice.

Epilogue

Live to Be Missed

I n 1945, Billy Graham wasn't the only young preacher who had a huge following. Have you ever heard the names Chuck Templeton or Bron Clifford? In 1945, Templeton and Clifford were getting even more attention than Billy Graham. In fact, one seminary president who heard Templeton preach called him the most talented young preacher in America.

Both Templeton and Graham ministered for an organization they helped found called Youth for Christ, which is still active today. Both were extraordinary preachers, and the pair even toured Western Europe together, holding evangelistic crusades in England, Scotland, Ireland, and other countries. They gained widespread attention among major evangelical Christian leaders.

But by 1957, Templeton had declared himself an agnostic, returned to Canada, went into politics, and then became a journalist. He published a book titled *Farewell to God: My Reasons for Rejecting the Christian Faith.*

And Bron Clifford? He went on to lose his family, his ministry, his health, and his life. The strongholds of alcohol and financial irresponsibility destroyed him. He left his wife and his two Down syndrome children, and at age thirty-five, he died of cirrhosis of the liver in a run-down hotel in Texas. His last job was selling used cars. He died, as one pastor put it, "unwept, unhonored, and unsung."[39]

And Billy Graham? You know how his story turned out.

Leave a Great Legacy

All of us have an opportunity to leave a legacy. We will all die one day. What will others say of us when our bodies are placed at the front of a church? I know what I want them to say about me: "This man was not perfect, but God did an amazing work in his life. He was a godly man. He left a great reputation. His life truly honored God."

Proverbs 10:7 declares, "The memory of the righteous is blessed, but the name of the wicked will rot."

While Billy Graham will leave a blessed memory, Chuck Templeton and Bron Clifford did not. What makes the difference between a revered name and a rotten one?

It all comes down to what you do with the flesh. How will you respond to temptation when it comes calling? How will you wear the armor of God and wield the weapons of God? What will you do when the enemy tries to build a stronghold in the center of your territory?

God has put a verse and a prayer in my heart for you. In Psalm 18:2, David wrote, "The LORD is my rock and my fortress and my deliverer; my God, my strength, in whom I will trust; my shield and the horn of my salvation, my stronghold."

That's the kind of stronghold I want in my life! It's also the kind of stronghold that I pray will be in yours. We all know that every man has a propensity to do foolish things that can get the best of him. It may start as a thought. It soon becomes a deed. Over time it morphs into a habit, and finally, it turns into a stronghold. We're all susceptible to that same ugly progression.

So here's my prayer. Instead of some stronghold of the enemy overcoming you and me, I pray that the Lord Himself will be our stronghold. If someone should ask me, "Johnny, do you have any strongholds in your life?" wouldn't it be awesome if I could say, honest before God, "My stronghold is the Lord"?

Throughout this book, we've seen that strongholds typically come from addictions to various weaknesses of the flesh. But not all addictions have to be bad. The apostle Paul once said of some friends that "they have devoted themselves to the ministry of the saints" (1 Corinthians 16:15). The word "devoted" speaks of an addiction. I would rather be addicted to serving Jesus than to pornography any day. I would like to go to heaven believing that I did so much for Jesus that I was addicted to Him.

I want Jesus to be my stronghold, gripping me so tightly I can't get loose. I want to be fully in his grasp. If you finish this book with an addiction, I pray it's an addiction to Jesus and to the ministry of the saints. I pray that you care deeply for the people Jesus has placed in your network and that you are loving and caring for them.

Let me encourage you to live today in such a way that when you're gone, you'll be deeply missed. Writer David Brooks has rightly encouraged us to focus on developing our "eulogy virtues" rather than our "résumé virtues." Chew on that one for a while.

You really *can* win. You *can* become a man of integrity. You *can* demolish the strongholds that have held you back for too long.

God *wants* you to succeed. He's *eager* for you to become the man of your dreams. As we close this book, recognize that what happens in this life is far bigger than just you or me. Much, *much* bigger.

The Rest of the Story

Remember my late friend, Bobby Apon, who let a stronghold of the enemy drive him to suicide? His earthly story ended at Lake Allatoona, but he left behind a widow and eight children. Would you like to know what's happened to them?

Shortly after his funeral, Bobby's whole family joined our church. My wife, Janet, and I chose to be heavily involved in trying to support them and send them to special events. A number of businessmen also got together, rallied support, and sent the family on ski trips and to Disney World. People in the church did whatever they could to show loving care.

Not long after that, I asked Dr. Jerry Falwell Jr. of Liberty University for a special favor. I then served on the board of the school, and he granted my request to give all eight kids a full scholarship to the university. Every one of them will have the opportunity to attend the largest Christian university in the world.

But that doesn't mean they don't miss their daddy! They miss him every day. Some time ago, Bobby's widow put together a video in which she and some of her children told part of their story. "I want to give you this," she told me, "and I want you to pray about using it." She and her kids created the video in the hopes that it might spare other families the kind of heartache they've had to endure. It's designed to help men avoid becoming casualties of the enemy, to awaken them to the grim reality of just how far the devil desires to take them. Strongholds are really Satan's death camps.

Bobby's widow starts out the sobering video by saying,

> I remember the night that I met Bobby. We started talking, and right away, there was an attraction there—but he was tall, dark, and handsome. He was my knight in shining armor, so I was a little bit leery. Could this really be true? The more we talked, the more I realized that he was deeply in love with Jesus. I left that concert so excited that night, and went home and told my roommate that I had met the man I was going to marry.
>
> He called me the next morning and told me that he had prayed and had asked God to let him marry me. And he said that if God let him marry me, he would be the

happiest man. I had no doubt that Bobby was the man
that God had hand-picked for me. Bobby never had any
doubt that I was the wife for him.

Sounds like a fairy tale, doesn't it? But like most fairy tales, this
one had a dark side. She continues:

> We came to our wedding altar, both of us really in bond-
> age, both of us prisoners of the enemy. I was in prison
> to an eating disorder and struggled with anorexia. I was
> captive to that, although I didn't know it. Bobby was in
> bondage to another form of addiction.
>
> Soon after we were married, we began to have children,
> and lots of them. They came really fast. About every year
> we would have another baby, another blessing.
>
> Over the course of time, Bobby made some choices that
> cost him his ministry, which he was required to leave. That
> was a real turning point, a real transition time in our family.

You already know the tragic part of the story, so I won't rehearse
that here. But I do want you to recognize that Bobby hadn't turned
into a monster. Rather, he had failed to deal ruthlessly with the
stronghold that kept him captive. Here's how his son remembers him:

> My dad was real involved in making sure I played sports as
> a little kid. I used to play Little League baseball, although
> I was never a good hitter. I still am not a very good hit-
> ter, but one time I got a hit, and he got *so* excited! He
> screamed at me, he was so excited for me to *run*. I didn't
> know what to do, so he ran out on the field, grabbed my
> hand, held it, and helped me run around the bases. I've
> never really forgotten that. It showed that he really did
> care for me, even in the little things. He truly loved me.

After Bobby's shocking death, the kids' mother gathered them together and told them that they had a new daddy. She quoted Psalm 68:5 to them: "A father of the fatherless, a defender of widows, is God in His holy habitation."

In the video, one of the children says, "God has been able to be a father to the fatherless through the different men that Mom has placed as mentors in my life." Another says, "I think a lot of what helped me transition from having a natural daddy to having a supernatural daddy was basically praying a lot. I would go to my room and cry and cry and cry until I couldn't cry anymore, and I would literally almost feel God wrapping me in His arms—just comforting me, and talking to me, and singing to me in a way that my real daddy used to do. It was that way the more I talked to God. And the more I would just cry and get all my grief out, God would keep coming over and over again and keep showing Himself real."

God has been faithful to these children. He has been their supernatural daddy, and He has graciously enabled people in our church to step into the gap and have a significant ministry to the whole family. I praise Him for that.

But what if Bobby had allowed God to help him tear down the stronghold that eventually choked the life out of him? What if he had chosen to put on his armor and tap into God's power to wield the weapons of spiritual warfare that God offers to all of us? What if he had learned to take *every* thought captive to the obedience of Christ?

Bobby's earthly story is over. But yours isn't! I pray that God would help you to make wise decisions that lead to life. Don't let an enemy stronghold make you into another casualty. God longs to help you. He offers you a way out of bondage, a way out of captivity, a way out of prison.

You really can be free, if you want to be. Make God your stronghold! And then prepare for the adventure of your life.

Appendix:

Key Scriptures for Persistent Strongholds

Psalms 32; 51

Proverbs 3:13-18

Proverbs 4:14-15

Proverbs 4:23

Proverbs 4:24-27

Proverbs 5; 6; 7

Proverbs 8:36

Proverbs 9:17-18

Proverbs 10:2-3

Proverbs 11:2-3

Proverbs 12:4

Proverbs 14:14,16

Proverbs 14:26-27

Proverbs 16:7

Proverbs 18:1,10,12,22

Proverbs 19:3,14

Proverbs 20:7 (my favorite)

Proverbs 20:17

Proverbs 22:8,11,14

Proverbs 23:7a,17

Proverbs 23:24-25
(I pray over my children)

Proverbs 24:10,16

Proverbs 25:26-28

Proverbs 26:11-12

Proverbs 27:5-6

Proverbs 27:17,19

Proverbs 28:13
(confessors must forsake!)

Proverbs 29:1

Proverbs 29:23

Proverbs 31:3

Proverbs 31
(especially verse 23)

Ecclesiastes 7:25-27

Ecclesiastes 9:9

Ecclesiastes 10:1

Ecclesiastes 12:14

Isaiah 57:20

Romans 12:1-2

Romans 13:14

1 Corinthians 6:9-11

1 Corinthians 6:15-20

2 Corinthians 2:11

2 Corinthians 11:2-3

Galatians 5:16-26

Galatians 6:1-2

Galatians 6:7-9

Ephesians 4:1-2

Ephesians 4:17-24

Ephesians 6:10-18

Philippians 4:8 (the best)

Philippians 4:13,19

Colossians 3:5-10

Colossians 3:15-17

1 Thessalonians 4:3

1 Thessalonians 5:19,23-24

1 Timothy 1:5

1 Timothy 3:7

1 Timothy 4:8,12,15

1 Timothy 6:9-10

1 Timothy 6:11-12

Titus 2:6-8

James 1:5

James 1:12-15 (temptation)

James 1:16,22,26 (deceived)

James 1:27

James 4:1-6

James 4:7-10

James 4:17

James 5:19-20

1 Peter 1:22

1 Peter 4:1-4

2 Peter 1:8-9

1 John 1:6-10
    (especially verse 9)

1 John 2:1-2

1 John 3:3

3 John 4 (my wife Janet's
    favorite verse)

Jude 24-25

Revelation 14:13

Notes

1. Kent Hughes, *The Disciplines of a Godly Man* (Wheaton, IL: Crossway, 2006), 72.

2. Oswald Chambers, *My Utmost for His Highest* (Grand Rapids, MI: Discovery House, 2012), April 19.

3. Jason Ranew, "It Does Matter Who Your Friends Are," August 13, 2005, *The Good News*, https://www.ucg.org/the-good-news/just-for-youth-it-does-matter-who-your-friends-are.

4. Ibid.

5. Ibid.

6. See chapter 11 in John Maxwell, *The 21 Irrefutable Laws of Leadership* (Nashville: Thomas Nelson, 2007).

7. Kiernan Hopkins, "Amanda's Story," October 24, 2015, http://distracteddriveraccidents.com/amandas-story/.

8. Ibid.

9. Ibid.

10. Jim Goad, "10 Grimly Ironic Texting-While-Driving Car Crashes," June 2014, Thoughtcatalog.com/jim-goad/2014/06/10-grimly-ironic-texting-while-driving-car-crashes.

11. Ibid.

12. See at http://www.roadtograce.net/current-porn-statistics/.

13. Oswald Chambers, *My Utmost for His Highest* (Grand Rapids, MI: Discovery House, 2012), December 28.

14. Ibid.

15. John Owen, *Overcoming Sin and Temptation*, ed. Justin Taylor (Wheaton, IL: Crossway, 2006), 194.

16. Erwin W. Lutzer, *Getting to No: How to Break a Stubborn Habit* (Colorado Springs: David C. Cook, 2010), 30.

17. George MacDonald, *Unspoken Sermons* (New York: Cosimo Classics, 2007), 401.

18. John Trapp, as cited by G. Campbell Morgan, *The Gospel According to Luke*, G. Campbell Morgan Reprint Series (Eugene, OR: Wipf and Stock, 2010), 247.

19. According to the National Institute on Alcohol Abuse and Alcoholism, 16.3 million adults were diagnosed as having Alcohol Use Disorder (AUD) in the United States per a 2014 survey. See at https://www.niaaa.nih.gov/alcohol-health/overview-alcohol-consumption/alcohol-facts-and-statistics.

20. This quote, frequently attributed to Robert Murray McCheyne, is said to have come from a letter he addressed to Reverend Dan Edwards, a missionary friend, in 1840.

21. "Porn Sites Get More Visitors Each Month Than Netflix, Amazon and Twitter Combined," *The Huffington Post*, May 4, 2013, http://www.huffingtonpost.com/2013/05/03/internet-porn-stats_n_3187682.html.

22. "Shocker: Study Shows Most Christian Men Are into Porn," *Charismanews*, October 7, 2014, http://www.charismanews.com/us/45671-shocker-study-shows-most-christian-men-are-into-porn.

23. John D. Rockefeller, quoted in Barry Morrow, *Yearning for More* (Carol Stream, IL: InterVarsity, 2012), 40.

24. John D. Rockefeller, quoted in *The N.C.R.*, H.M. Hyde, ed. (Dayton, OH: National Cash Register Co., 1897), vol. X, 206.

25. As cited in Randy C. Alcorn, *Money, Possessions, and Eternity* (Wheaton, IL: Tyndale, 2003), 47.

26. Dan Grover, "The Antidote to Materialism," https://www.ronblue.com/Library/Article/the-antidote-to-materialism-454.

27. C.S. Lewis, *Mere Christianity* (Grand Rapids, MI: Zondervan, 2001), 122.

28. Ibid.

29. Ibid.

30. As cited by Jerry Bridges in *The Pursuit of Holiness* (Colorado Springs: NavPress, 1978), 20.

31. Alexander Maclaren, *The Psalms* (New York: A.C. Armstrong and Son, 1905), 305.

32. Oswald Chambers, *Biblical Psychology* (Grand Rapids, MI: Discovery House, 2014), Kindle edition.

33. As cited in Bruce Wilkinson, *30 Days to Discovering Personal Victory Through Holiness* (Sisters, OR: Multnomah, 2003), Kindle edition.

34. As cited in Bruce Wilkinson, *30 Days to Discovering Personal Victory Through Holiness* (Sisters, OR: Multnomah, 2003), Kindle edition.

35. Proverbs 20:7.

36. Beth Moore, *Praying God's Word* (Nashville: B&H Books, 2009), 5. Emphasis in original.

37. Dietrich Bonhoeffer, *Life Together* (New York: HarperOne, 2009), 110-11.

38. Oswald Chambers, *Biblical Psychology* (Grand Rapids, MI: Discovery House, 2014), Kindle version.

39. As cited by Steve Farrar, *Finishing Strong* (Colorado Springs: Multnomah, 1995), 15. This story is told in Farrar's book as well.

Other Good Books by Harvest House Publishers

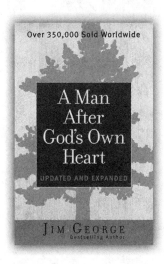

A Man After God's Own Heart
Jim George

Many Christian men want to be men after God's own heart...but how do they do this? Bestselling author Jim George shares God's perfect design for how you can become this kind of man:

- *your life example*—letting others see God in your words and actions
- *your work*—modeling integrity and diligence in the workplace
- *your church*—discovering how and where God can ue you
- *your marriage*—what it means to love, lead, and protect your wife
- *your children*—the keys to training them up and shaping their hearts

Commit to becoming a man after God's own heart. Following God's priorities is the most rewarding pursuit ever!

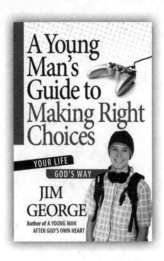

A Young Man's Guide to Making Right Choices
Jim George

Making right choices is a constant challenge for teen guys! Where can you go for answers? Jim George shares principles from God's Word that will guide you toward making right decisions today and in the future—decisions on how to...

- make the best kinds of friends
- stand strong for what's right and succeed
- resist temptation and avoid bad situations
- get along better with your family
- set standards for your friendships with girls

In this great resource for developing crucial decision-making skills, you'll learn how to make the choices that give you the confidence, wisdom, and strength to live your life God's way.

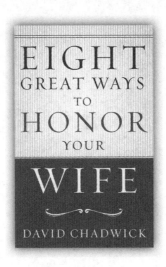

Eight Great Ways to Honor Your Wife
David Chadwick

What does it mean to honor your wife?

God calls you not only to love your wife, but also to honor her. Sadly, honor is a missing ingredient in many marriages today.

Love and honor practiced together will take your marriage to a whole new level. Join author David Chadwick as he shares eight great ways to make this happen:

trust her instincts	share your heart
be a man of God	read her well
encourage her gifts	be a guardian and gardener
use words wisely	ask a certain question often

Make honoring your wife an everyday part of your life—and experience the very best of what God can do in your marriage relationship!

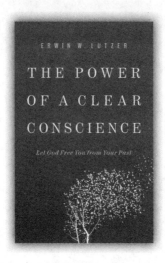

The Power of a Clear Conscience
Erwin W. Lutzer

Do you struggle with feelings of guilt about your past? Or are you bogged down by a conscience that haunts or imprisons you?

This is not how God intends for you to live. Your conscience was not created to hold you prisoner, but to guide you and point you to freedom from guilt and bad habits. It's designed to tell you the truth so you are not held in bondage to lies or sin. A clear conscience enables you to live in the present without being distracted, mentally or emotionally, by your past.

In *The Power of a Clear Conscience*, you'll…

- learn how to deal with guilt and replace it with joy
- discover how the truth that can hurt you can also heal you
- realize the incredible extent of God's forgiveness and love for you

You'll find yourself encouraged by the truths that no failure is permanent and no life is beyond God's power to bring about change.

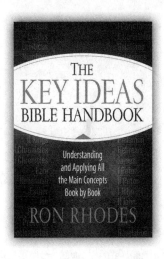

The Key Ideas Bible Handbook
Ron Rhodes

From Genesis to Revelation, the Bible is full of life-changing truth. But to fully experience the power of God's Word, you can go beyond merely knowing the facts—you can let them transform you.

In this unique resource, noted author and Bible scholar Ron Rhodes takes you through each book of the Bible, breaking down complex concepts into practical applications and offering helpful insights for each.

Word studies, quotes from famous Christians, cross-references, and more are included in every profound chapter to help you dig deeper into each transformational concept. As you put God's key principles into practice, you'll experience more than ever all the benefits the Bible has to offer.

To learn more about Harvest House books and
to read sample chapters, visit our website:

www.harvesthousepublishers.com

HARVEST HOUSE PUBLISHERS
EUGENE, OREGON